Vail

STORY OF A COLORADO MOUNTAIN VALLEY

DEDICATION

This book is for Don and Cliff and Denny
And for my father, Elliot Clifford Bergen

A SPECIAL ACKNOWLEDGMENT

to SUSIE KINCADE and FRANK W. MARTIN, without whose faith and guidance this book would never have been completed.

CONTENTS

Published by: Taylor Publishing Company
Produced by: W. Fuller, Jr.
Frank W. Martin, Editorial Consultant
Susie Kincade, Marketing Director
Laurie Musick Wright, Designer
David Lokey, Photographer

Printed in the United States of America by
Taylor Publishing Company, Dallas, Texas.
First Edition

ISBN #— 0-87833-603-6

Vail

STORY OF A COLORADO MOUNTAIN VALLEY

BY JUNE SIMONTON

THE FINEBOOKS DIVISION OF
TAYLOR PUBLISHING COMPANY, DALLAS

 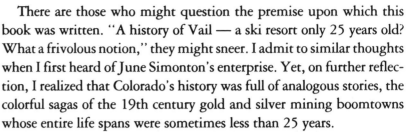

INTRODUCTION

There are those who might question the premise upon which this book was written. "A history of Vail — a ski resort only 25 years old? What a frivolous notion," they might sneer. I admit to similar thoughts when I first heard of June Simonton's enterprise. Yet, on further reflection, I realized that Colorado's history was full of analogous stories, the colorful sagas of the 19th century gold and silver mining boomtowns whose entire life spans were sometimes less than 25 years.

Now, upon reading June's fascinating narrative, I realize that she has known all along that the story of Vail is, in effect, telescoped, encapsulated history. Like the stories of Apex, Aspen, Creede, Cripple Creek, Holy Cross, Kokomo, Montezuma, and Tin Cup, Vail's 25 years, as well as the pioneer years that preceded the resort's founding, are jam-packed with the stuff of history: heroes and villains, victories and defeats, artists and athletes, crises and confrontations, clowns, congressmen, weddings, funerals, politics, and pollution.

Many of the traditional themes of the building of a pioneer community are present here, with the obvious exception that Vail, unlike most of the lumber and mining boomtowns, is a thriving, ongoing community based on that wonderful renewable resource, snow, rather than a silent ghost town whose very life depended on resources soon dug up or cut down.

Other skeptics might be tempted to question whether Vail, as a "mountain retreat for the idle rich," deserved to be dignified by an historical treatise, no matter how entertaining. On this score, it is time to apply a newer perspective. In today's America, outdoor recreation, including all the sports activities that Vail offers, has become not a luxury but a basic necessity in our progressively more air-conditioned, computerized, and mechanized society.

No community could have a more honorable *raison d'etre* than that of providing healthful, family-oriented recreation in the inspiring setting of the high Rockies to thousands of Americans whose lives are otherwise subject to increasingly larger daily doses of pollution, stress, societal regimentation, and stultifying, push-button environment.

History will judge whether Vail will exist substantively longer than Colorado's other boomtowns. Until that judgement has been rendered, let's be grateful that we have the chance, thanks to June Simonton, to share in the sometimes outrageous, often incredible but always entertaining history of this "instant Austria," this "synthetic Switzerland," this uniquely indigenous 20th century phenomenon known as Vail, Colorado, Ski Country U.S.A.

Robert W. Parker
Senior Vice President (Retired)
Vail Associates, Inc.
Vail, Colorado

OREWORD

When I first brought my family to Vail in 1968, we were all impressed by the beauty of the Colorado Rockies. That beauty added a special dimension to the sport of skiing. It was wonderful exercise in a magnificent environment, and it regenerated not just muscles but mind and spirit as well. Today, in our complex world, we need this kind of total recreation; we need the opportunity to recreate our strength and our vision, so easily eroded by the pressures of everyday living. Recreation has become an important part of the American scene and the American spirit.

Full-time residents in a resort like Vail are deeply involved in this industry of recreation, and very few people have any idea how hard they work at it. Hundreds of people are needed to make all facets of a resort run smoothly. In the valley and on the mountain, work goes on behind the scenes 24 hours a day. The jobs are challenging, exciting, sometimes dangerous, and they are all geared toward providing the visitor with a safe, happy recreational experience.

Betty and I have come to know many of these people over the years. We have seen incredible changes in Vail as it grew from a small ski area into a resort of international renown. We are pleased to have participated in that development.

But we have seen another important change. We have seen Vail grow into a very real human community where babies are born and children grow up and adults contend with ordinary pressures of life under the challenging circumstances that mountain living often brings. It is this community of people working together in a beautiful mountain resort that makes for Vail's special recreational appeal.

This book describes the history of our Vail Valley and our neighbors who live and work there. I know you will find their stories interesting.

Gerald R. Ford
38th President of the United States

8

The Land

of the

Shining

Mountains

———◆———

I

VAIL WAS BORN in a sheep pasture at the foot of an unnamed mountain, where a two-lane road meandered along Gore Creek past a few sagging barns and homestead cabins.

Some in the ski world thought Vail an upstart. Aspen called it a storybook village; others labeled it instant alpine, transplanted Tyrolea, Swiss schmaltz. But Vail's timing was perfect. In that year of 1962, America was hooked on skiing — and skiers fell in love with Vail.

"Never has a mountain leaped in such a short time into the four-star category of ski resorts," declared *Sports Illustrated* in 1964. "The sheer scale, variety and general excellence of skiable terrain are somewhat staggering," echoed the *Chicago Sun-Times.*

News of Vail spread like gold rush fever. Olympic skiers arrived, followed by congressmen, college kids, rock stars, secretaries, doctors, lawyers, and corporate chiefs. New chairlifts and new trails opened up on the mountain. Condominiums and houses sprouted in the valley. The golf course expanded to 18 holes and conventioneers arrived by the busload.

Fame sparked curiosity. Reporters, rounding out articles, often asked about the Gore Creek Valley. Did gold strikes, cattle drives, or railroad barons figure in its past? Not at all. Vail, it seemed, was an orphan with nothing to nail it into place in the pattern of Western history. Its valley, a high and lonely twist of land cut off at one end by a 10,600 foot pass and at the other by a canyon barely horse-width wide, was a blank spot on early Colorado maps. The course of 19th century exploration swirled all around the Gore Creek Valley, but little went through it.

In the nearby mountains, however, four men left their mark — John Wesley Powell, Ferdinand V. Hayden, William Henry Jackson, and Thomas Moran. All associated with the Great Surveys of the American West, they passed through this area during a brief period of history between 1868 and 1879. They dug no holes, built no fences, staked no claims. Yet these men greatly influenced the development of Colorado and played out their stories against the background of another story — the sad tale of the Ute Indians.

During the second half of the 19th century, the United States government claimed land in the West under Manifest Destiny, a doctrine which asserted the right of Americans "to overspread the continent alloted by Providence for the free development of our yearly multiplying millions."

Colorado's Ute Indians knew nothing about Manifest Destiny. They simply knew that the land had been theirs forever, whether Providence had alloted it or not. They viewed the earth with reverence; the land, they said, was the body and the people were its spirit. They called their Colorado homeland The Shining Mountains.

The watercolor shown on page 8 was painted by Thomas Moran in Manitou Springs, Colorado, as a wedding gift for Cora Rowena Bell, who married Harold Pearce in 1894. The painting went with the Pearces when they moved to England. In 1981 Colorado relatives of the family bought the painting and donated it to the Denver Art Museum. (Photo Courtesy of the Denver Art Museum)

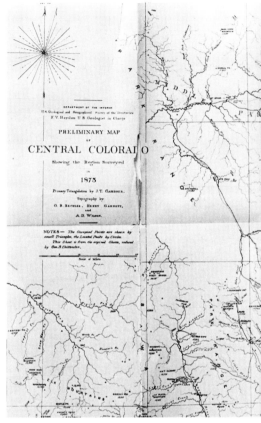

A portion of a map in F. V. Hayden's book reporting his survey of Colorado Territory. Mt. Powell and "Mountain of the Holy Cross" are clearly located, but only a blank spot indicates the Gore Creek Valley between them. Surveyors of the Hayden Survey, left, map a section of the Rockies after the Civil War. (Colorado Historical Society Photo)

Born in 1833 and raised in Taos, New Mexico, Ouray understood both the red and the white civilizations. Trusted by the Utes for his wisdom and honesty, he was also admired by Washington politicians, who treated him royally when he visited the East. Members of the Hayden Survey, bottom, throw a diamond hitch over the load of one of their pack mules. (Colorado Historical Society Photos)

The Utes held sacred not only their land but also the tough and beautiful pinto ponies they had bred for generations. Their acquisition of horses had turned the Utes from half-starved primitive wanderers into bold and skillful hunters and traders. By the middle of the 19th century, they owned thousands of horses. They also owned almost all of Colorado west of the Continental Divide.

The Utes moved with the seasons across a land ripe with game and grass. They saw few white men and had no quarrel with them. But time was growing short for these Indians in their mountain homeland. Under the flag of Manifest Destiny, white civilization surged over the mountain passes and out along the rivers onto land that belonged to the Utes.

The presence of strangers disturbed the Utes, but Ouray, their chief, wanted peace. He signed treaties with the government guaranteeing the friendship of his people in return for promises that portions of Colorado would belong to the Utes forever. But when white men found gold on Ute land, the government went back to Ouray with more treaty papers and more promises until he finally realized that treaties with white men had no more substance than a mountain breeze. The treaties guaranteed nothing.

After the Civil War, Congress allocated funds to explore, for the sake of science, what lay beyond its frontiers. Geologists, entomologists, ornithologists, paleontologists, ethnologists, topographers, journalists, photographers, and artists packed their odometers, transits, notebooks, and sketchpads and headed out in expeditions known as the Great Surveys of the American West.

The surveyors traversed vast stretches of the new land with its deep canyons, shimmering peaks, and lavender-green valleys. They endured windstorms, duststorms, snowsqualls, sunburn, and saddle sores. They froze at hasty timberline camps, survived for weeks on beans and biscuits, narrowly escaped forest fires and irate Indians, and coped with the evil tempers of their government mules.

Some surveyors received good pay for their services while others barely got by. John Wesley Powell, a poor lobbyist in Congress, sometimes borrowed money to fund his expeditions. A brilliant scientist and coura-

As seen from Vail Mountain, Mt. Powell, top, is the summit on the right. (Photo by David Lokey) Major John Wesley Powell, head of the Geographical and Geological Survey of the Rocky Mountain Region, lost his right arm in the Civil War Battle of Shiloh in 1862. This handicap did not prevent him from climbing mountains and scaling canyon walls on his explorations of Colorado and Utah. (Colorado Historical Society Photo)

THE RESCUE.

*D*rawing, left, from Powell's book, "The Exploration of the Colorado River and Its Canyons," illustrates the courage of the one-armed man, stranded while climbing cliffs above the Green River. A friend rescued him. (Dover Books) Above, Powell with Paiute Indian in Utah. (Colorado Historical Society Photo)

geous man who lost his right arm in a Civil War battle, Powell led his second survey into the Rocky Mountains in 1868.

His survey party made one of the first ascents of Longs Peak in the Front Range and then struck out across the northern part of the territory to a winter camp on the White River. To the south, Powell saw the stunning crags of the Gore Range. Never one to pass up a challenge, he and two other men left the survey party to try for the highest peak in the range.

On a snowfield near the top of the mountain, they discovered three grizzly bears lunching on grasshoppers. In days of grasshopper plagues, clouds of the insects often drifted east over the Rocky Mountains, died in the cold air, and fell onto the snow to provide high altitude snacks for the bears. After seeing the bears, Powell continued to the mountaintop, finding the climb "difficult and tedious," but the view of the surrounding country well worth it. Later, at their camp, a newspaper correspondent with the party described Powell's adventure in the Gore Range and named the mountain after him.

While Powell enjoyed mountains, rivers intrigued him even more, and in 1869, he gained fame for his harrowing adventures on the Green and Colorado Rivers and into the wilderness of the Grand Canyon, an exploration that offered more thrills per mile than any man could want, let alone a man with only one arm.

For all his thrill-seeking, Powell remained observant and thoughtful, a man keenly sensitive to his environment. He understood the essentially arid nature of the West and knew that its development would depend on the availability of water. In his "Report on the Lands of the Arid Region," Powell proposed land-use studies and urged Congress to plan carefully for the future of the West. But Congress, pressured by development interests, ignored his advice.

Shunned at times by congressmen, Powell found himself well accepted among the Indians of Colorado and Utah. The Shoshones called him "Ka'purats," which meant "arm-off," and welcomed him on their land even at a time when they felt increasing pressure from white men.

"We will give you food when you come to our land," the Indians told Powell. "We will show you the springs and you may drink; the water is good. We will tell the Indians who live on the other side of the river that we have seen Ka'purats, and that he is the Indian's friend."

Ferdinand Vandiveer Hayden, another Great Survey leader, wangled congressional funding with golden-tongued oratory and kept his surveys well-financed from 1867 to 1879. Photographer William Henry Jackson and artist Thomas Moran explored the Yellowstone with Hayden, and if his oratorical lobbying fell short, he had only to produce Jackson's photographs and Moran's paintings to kindle interest in his projects. The Hayden party foray into Wyoming territory convinced Congress to set aside the Yellowstone country as a national park in 1872.

In the summer of 1873, Hayden and Jackson turned their attention to the rugged mountains of the Colorado territory, determined, among other things, to find the exact location of the Mount of the Holy Cross.

Lost among the tangled peaks of the Sawatch Range, the Mount of the Holy Cross had never been climbed and only rarely seen. On the mountain's face, nature had carved a vertical fissure 1,500 feet high

Dr. Ferdinand Vandiveer Hayden on his horse, Patsy. Hayden directed the United States Geological and Geographical Survey of the Territories from 1869 to 1878. Sioux Indians called the geologist-surveyor "man-who-picks-up-stones-running." (Denver Public Library, Western History Department Photo)

Lord Gore

The mountains forming the horizon north of Vail took their name from one of Colorado's most bizarre tourists, Sir St. George Gore an Irishman who led an extravagantly equipped hunting party on a three-year outing through the American West, devastated the local wildlife, and dropped $250,000 into the frontier economy along the way. A mountain range, a pass, a peak, a canyon, and two streams bear his name. So does Vail's Gore Creek Valley, although he never set foot in it.

Nicknamed Lord Gore, he was not actually royalty but rather a wealthy baronet from Sligo, Ireland, who sailed to America in January, 1854, and arrived in St. Louis in March to make final preparations for his hunt.

To assure his personal comfort, Gore packed a green and white silk tent with carpeted floor, a bathtub, a brass bedstead, a down mattress, linens, lamps, leather-bound versions of his favorite classics, pewter mugs, plates, and candlesticks, and for chilly mountain mornings, a commode with a fur-lined seat.

Gore planned to smooth his way through Indian country with trade goods — knives, tools, cheap guns, mirrors, beads, yards of cloth, and 250 gallons of 180-proof grain alcohol. Diluted and flavored with red pepper and plug tobacco, the alcohol turned into a poisonous brew known as trade whiskey. Cowboy artist Charlie Russell once remarked: "If you could drink trade whiskey, you could get shot and killed, but you wouldn't die 'til you sobered up."

In the middle of June, St. Louis residents watched in awe as Lord

Gore assembled his baggage. Four Conestoga wagons carried food, cooking equipment and tools, two huge freight wagons with eight-foot sides hauled supplies in crates and boxes, and 16 "Red River" carts, especially designed for mountain travel, carried the baronet's personal possessions, including a collection of shooting irons custom-made by England's finest gunsmiths.

With dozens of servants and workmen, 100 horses, 20 yokes of oxen, and 50 hunting hounds, the unwieldy caravan unfolded itself onto the dusty Oregon Trail with Lord Gore riding comfortably in a padded carriage, accompanied by the famous mountain man Jim Bridger, who had been hired as guide.

The hunting party established a late summer base camp at Fort Laramie, and from there Gore made a foray into what would become Colorado's North Park, a huge grassy valley filled with deer, elk, antelope, and great herds of buffalo. Throughout the weeks of autumn, Gore and his friends chased and shot every four-footed creature within range. They took only trophies and left the rest to rot.

Each evening after the hunt, Gore relaxed in his silk tent where servants heated bath water, lit the lanterns, and uncorked the wine. Jim Bridger often entertained the Irishman with frontier yarns, and Gore, in turn, opened his leather-bound books and read excerpts from William Shakespeare, Sir Walter Scott, and Robert Burns. Shakespeare caught Bridger's fancy and legend had it that, years later, Bridger located a book of Shakespeare's works in a wagon train, traded a yoke of oxen for it, and hired at boy at $40 a month to read it to him.

Gore's expedition continued north through Wyoming and into Montana and the Dakotas, where he ravaged thousands of buffalo, elk, deer, and bear, and uncounted smaller animals.

Word about the wild Irishman leaked into remote wilderness villages where native Americans solemnly noted the depletion of their food supply. Washington, D.C. officials heard about the hunt and made plans to oust the baronet as soon as they could get their hands on him.

Gore reached Fort Union on the upper Missouri River where he planned to sell his animals and equipment, buy rafts, and float down the Missouri to St. Louis. But negotiations went badly and Gore, in a fit of rage, piled up his carts, wagons, the silk tent, all his elegant possessions, and set a torch to them.

He then took his hounds and horses, a few provisions, and a dozen men and headed out for one last hunt into the Black Hills, alien Indian territory. On a day in October, Gore crossed the trail of Bear's Rib, an irritable Uncpapa Sioux, whose war party surrounded Gore and his men, stripped them of their horses and supplies and every last stitch of clothing they wore, and strongly suggested that they leave the country.

Thus ended the saga of the arrogant Lord Gore, who set forth with an entourage unmatched in the history of the American West and ended up wandering naked in the wilderness, grubbing for roots. Friendly Hidatsa Indians found him and gave him shelter for the winter.

The following spring, Sir St. George Gore quietly made his way home to Ireland. ■

with arms 750 feet wide, a cross perpetually filled with snow.

Romance and legend wrapped the hidden mountain in mystery with tales of lost and starving men suddenly seeing the cross through rifts in the clouds and finding their way out of the wilderness, and with tales of lovers searching for one another on the mountain's slopes. Those stories so appealed to pious Americans that they viewed the mountain as a national shrine. Jackson promised his bride-to-be a photograph of it as a wedding gift.

Nineteenth century photography required a clear head, a strong back, and the soul of an optimist. When Jackson arrived each summer for the survey, he brought 300 pounds of equipment with him, including 400 glass plates in two sizes, 6 x 8 and 11 x 14 inches. With enlarging unknown at the time, cameras had to be big enough to accommodate the plates and mules strong and steady enough to carry cameras, plates, tripods, chemicals, kegs of water, and portable darkrooms.

To take a photograph, Jackson first covered a glass plate with a sensitizing chemical, inserted it into a wooden holder, and fitted the holder into the camera. With the camera on its tripod and properly aimed, he removed the cap from the lens, counted the seconds of exposure time, replaced the cap, pulled out the plate, and hurried into his darkroom tent to spread a fixing solution on the glass. Jackson learned the ropes of wilderness photography so well he could unpack his equipment, sensitize, load, expose, and fix the plate in 15 minutes flat.

Prior to the Holy Cross expedition, Jackson spent weeks capturing mountains on his glass plates. Then, on a rutted mountain trail, a mule named Gimlet lost his footing, slipped his pack, and broke almost all

William Henry Jackson, facing page, born in 1843, became an artist before taking up photography. He and his brother owned a studio in Omaha, Nebraska, when Ferdinand Hayden stopped by to convince Jackson to accompany him on his surveys of the West. Members of the Photographic Division of the Hayden Survey line up, above, with their saddle horses, while pack mules wait in the background. (Colorado Historical Society Photos)

the newly exposed plates. "Evil mule!" wrote Jackson. "I think I have never been so distressed in my life — my finest negatives lost before anyone had ever seen a print." Jackson recovered his composure, repacked the animal, and retraced his route to take the photographs all over again.

In late summer, Jackson, Hayden, and six other men crossed Tennessee Pass north of Leadville and camped in a broad, flat valley near the source of the Eagle River. Several men in the party climbed a nearby ridge and spotted the Mount of the Holy Cross, only eight miles away. The following day they probed the narrow Eagle River canyon, but sheer cliffs on both sides of the river forced them to traverse across the high slopes of Battle Mountain. That obstacle seemed slight compared to the next one.

Between the men and the mountain they sought lay a valley of *roches moutonnées,* or sheep-rocks — rounded, glaciated boulders from 10 to 50 feet high — that looked from a distance like flocks of sheep. Hundreds of fallen lodgepole pines tangled the spaces between the rocks.

"The obstacles to travel were very great," wrote Hayden. "We often labored for a day or two to find some path to approach the mountain peak and were obliged to cut our way through the fallen timber and finally succeeded in getting within about five miles of the base of the peak."

Once there, the party split. Hayden took three men with him to try for the summit while Jackson and two others unpacked the mules, divided the photographic equipment among themselves, and started up the boulder-strewn ridge of Notch Mountain hoping for a good view

Facing page, nineteenth century photography required that the darkroom go right into the wilderness with the photographer. Here, William Henry Jackson examines a glass plate outside his darkroom tent. Hayden and his survey party, above, camped along the Eagle River just before climbing the Mount of the Holy Cross. (Colorado Historical Society and U.S. Geological Survey Photos)

of the cross of snow.

Jackson pulled ahead of his friends on the long climb, scrambling higher and higher through fog that enveloped the ridge. "Near the top of the ridge I emerged above timberline and the clouds," he later wrote, "and suddenly, as I climbed over a vast mass of jagged rocks, I discovered the great shining cross before me, tilted against the mountainside."

Jackson's men arrived too late for photographs. Mist and clouds obscured the view and darkness caught them above timberline. Across the deep valley, they saw the tiny light of Hayden's campfire on the Mount of the Holy Cross. According to a correspondent with Hayden, "Both parties were compelled, instead of returning to camp, to do the best they could at timberline, with no wraps and only the lunch they had taken in their pockets, and had to finish their work on the following morning. Fortunately, the night was neither windy nor cold but 30 hours with no provisions but a pocket lunch was pretty hard on the men, some of whom had done 5,000 feet of climb with 30 or 40 pounds of instruments on their backs."

The following morning dawned clear, and William Henry Jackson took his photographs, using the melt-water he found in a rock depression for liquid to process the glass plates.

Meanwhile, Hayden's men took their topographical measurements, and then both parties made their tedious descents. "The Mount of the Holy Cross has been thoroughly done at last," wrote the correspondent, "but at a cost of time and labor that was not anticipated. It may be only after years, if at all, that another party will try to repeat the ascent."

But it was scarcely a year later that English artist Thomas Moran climbed Notch Mountain. Moran, who accompanied Hayden and Jackson into the Yellowstone region and Powell to the Grand Canyon, had gained national fame with his paintings of those grand American scenes. He heard about the Mount of the Holy Cross from Jackson, and he decided to see the mountain for himself.

Jackson greatly admired Moran, a frail man who rode horseback with a pillow on the saddle. "Prior to 1871, Moran had never known a true wilderness, and he was as poorly equipped for rough life as anyone I have ever known," said Jackson, "but it made no difference. He had so much to give and he gave so unstintingly that even a mountain or a waterfall must have responded to his charm. Moran became greatly interested in photography, and it was my good fortune to have him at my side during all that season to help me solve my problems of composition."

Moran struggled through the jumbled rock and timberfall of the *roches moutonnées* for three days. "Of all the hard climbing I have had, this beat it," he wrote to his wife. But when he reached the top of the ridge, "The view was perfectly magnificent. Two thousand feet below

A rendering from the Hayden Survey book shows the "roches moutonneés" or sheep-rocks, that made travel up Cross Creek almost impossible with mules and camping equipment. These glaciated boulders can be seen today from the highway on Battle Mountain south of Minturn.

Artist Thomas Moran and party, above, enroute to Notch Mountain to view the Mount of the Holy Cross in 1874. Moran is in front of the tent at right. (Denver Public Library, Western History Department Photo) Turn of the century photographer H. L. Standley took the photo of himself and his camera shown on pages 24 and 25 by stepping on a bulb which released the shutter. He is standing near the spot on Notch Mountain where Jackson had taken his famous 1873 pictures. (Collection of Fred and Jo Mazzulla, Courtesy of Robert L. Brown)

us lay the Moutonnées Valley with the Holy Cross Creek rushing through it, and at the head of the valley the splendid peak of the Holy Cross."

The following day Moran and his friends trudged slowly up the long ridge that Jackson climbed the year before. Sustained by cornbread, sardines, and a bottle of German wine, they climbed high enough to see the Mount of the Holy Cross. Moran sat quietly, absorbing its visual impact. Later, at his studio, with Jackson's photographs as references, he made many paintings of the mountain, using both oils and watercolors. He gave one small watercolor painting as a wedding gift to friends in Manitou Springs, Colorado.

With studious reports and glowing orations and with finely composed photographs and vivid paintings, Powell, Hayden, Jackson, and Moran took images of the new land back home. Those images sold the West.

"No longer do Americans need to cross the Atlantic," wrote railroad agent F.C. Nims, "and climb the frosty sides of Mont Blanc or gaze down the rock-riven slopes of Chamonix, to gratify the love for the grand and romantic in nature, which is implanted in every heart; for here we have loftier than alpine peaks, whose crests shine with the eternal snows, and vales of beauty which the best of old Europe cannot surpass."

New York Tribune Correspondent Bayard Taylor, who toured the Colorado territory in 1868, wrote, "It will be a national blessing when this region is open to general travel. Therefore, I am doubly glad I have come now, while there are still buffalo and danger of Indians on the plains, campfires to build in the mountains, and landscapes that have never yet been described."

Colorado captured the heart of the nation. Fortune hunters, land seekers, and tourists poured into the state. They crossed its eastern plains, passed through Denver and Colorado Springs, and eased their way into the mountains. Some hunted gold, some homesteaded, some merely admired the scenery and returned east to tell their friends about it.

All that spelled trouble for Colorado's natives. The white man did not understand that the high country belonged to the Utes. By 1879, Chief Ouray's dream of peace and friendship with white men hung in precarious balance. Denver politicians considered the Indians a nuisance and made plans to remove them entirely from the state. Unfortunately, the Utes played right into their hands.

On the White River Indian Reservation, where John Wesley Powell had wintered 10 years earlier, the Utes were following their traditional ways, hunting and trading throughout the high country and staging horse races for pleasure. They grazed hundreds of horses on the reservation and built a fine race track.

Nathan Meeker, a 60-year-old government agent, hoped to prepare the Utes for life among the white man by demonstrating the satisfactions of farming. With pathetic sincerity, he tried to convince them to give up their prized ponies and foolish horse racing and their wandering, wasteful ways.

Meeker simply did not understand that the Utes used the land in ways different from the white man. They wandered with the seasons in search of food and warmth, and graze for their ponies. They did not dig, or plant, or plow, or live in rectangular houses surrounded by rows of vegetables. The Utes pitied Meeker and tried to accommodate him without surrendering their cultural heritage. They remained friendly to his family and to other white families on the reservation and were so taken by two of the white children that they offered to buy them at a good price. But time ran out for everyone at the White River Reservation in 1879.

That year it rained only once in the spring and hardly at all during the summer. By July, forest fires were burning all over the state.

The fires delighted politicians in Denver. "Utes set spite fires!" they cried. The Utes angrily denied the charges, and Chief Nacaagat traveled from the reservation to Denver to explain that the Utes had not set any fires. By the end of the summer, though, a campaign against the Utes flared in newspaper headlines: "The Utes Must Go!"

Ouray objected. "We were born in the mountains and cannot change our abode like the white man. If we cannot live there, we will die there like brave men, with arms in our hands."

At the end of September, Nathan Meeker lost patience with his Utes and ordered their pastureland plowed up. The Utes warned away the plowman with rifle shots. Chief Canalla found Meeker at the agency office and told him to stop the plowing. Meeker refused and added the ultimate insult. "You have too many horses," he told Canalla. "You had better kill some of them."

Canalla grabbed Meeker, dragged him outside, and threw him against a hitching post. Meeker, badly frightened, called in troopers from Wyoming. When the Utes heard what he had done, they went north to defend their reservation border at Milk Creek. Neither the troopers nor the Utes really wanted to fight, but someone fired a shot by mistake and the week-long battle that followed left 100 men dead

*N*athan Meeker, 60 years old in the spring of 1879, hoped to prepare the Utes for life among the white man. He moved to the White River Reservation as Indian agent, but his misunderstanding of Indian ways dashed his hopes and led to his death. (Colorado Historical Society Photo)

*P*ainting, above, by an unknown artist depicts the Meeker Massacre at the White River Indian Reservation in September, 1879. (Colorado Historical Society Photo) When news of the Meeker Massacre arrived, citizens of the town of Red Cliff fortified a rock in the middle of town, naming it Fort Arnett, facing page. Judging by the jaunty poses, the scare had passed by the time this picture was taken. (Denver Public Library, Western History Department Photo)

or wounded. Back at the agency, the Utes killed Meeker and six other white men.

Ouray, who tried to stop the fighting, spoke wearily, "I do not want to be chief. I grow old and am tottering. Let some young man with the fire of youth in his veins take my place. I want only to be known as Ouray, the friend of the white man." He died just a few months before the Army gathered up the last of the Utes and forced them out of their Shining Mountains onto land in Utah that no one else wanted. Colorado's high country lay open to the white man.

The same dry weather that caused forest fires in 1879 also kept the snowpack low enough so railroad man William Loveland could blast a new wagon road over the Continental Divide for westward bound homesteaders.

The Great Surveys also ended in 1879, and Congress chose John Wesley Powell as chief of the newly-formed United States Geological Survey. Ferdinand Hayden received honorary degrees from two universities and a resolution of thanks from the Colorado legislature for his contributions to the state.

Thomas Moran's huge oil painting, "The Mountain of the Holy Cross," won a gold medal at the Centennial Exposition in Philadelphia. The tiny watercolor he painted as a wedding present went off to England with the bride and groom.

William Henry Jackson's popular photographs were reproduced as prints and postcards and in magazines and albums. In 1879, Henry Wadsworth Longfellow, romantic advocate of the American Indian, looked through one of those albums and saw Jackson's photograph of the Mount of the Holy Cross. Longfellow, still grieving over his wife's death, was so touched by the picture that he wrote these wistful words in tribute to his wife and to a Colorado vista he had never seen:

"There is a mountain in the distant west
That, sun-defying, in its deep ravines
Reveals a cross of snow upon its side.
Such is the cross I wear upon my breast
These eighteen years, through all the changing scenes
And seasons, changeless since the day she died."

The photograph of the mountain became as famous as the mountain itself. Although Jackson returned many times to the Mount of the Holy Cross, his later photographs never matched the ones he took that summer with the Hayden Survey in the Land of Shining Mountains.

*T*he life of William Henry Jackson ran parallel to the first century of photography. He is shown, facing page, with a 35mm camera in August, 1938. Jackson lived into his 99th year, riding a horse regularly until a back injury at 94 took him out of the saddle. He died in 1942, the year the 10th Mountain Division's Camp Hale began operations in the Pando Valley, where Jackson had camped on his quest for the Mount of the Holy Cross. (Denver Public Library, Western History Department Photo)

HOMESTEAD

STORIES

◆

II

A S THE UTES LOST GROUND in Colorado, the white man dug in. Those who found no gold or silver hired out to those who did. But after months of grubbing underground for someone else's gold, the hired miners simply yearned for clean fresh air and land to call their own. As one pioneer put it, "Them people stayed in the mines 'til they lost their health, which didn't take too long with all that dust and no modern machinery nor nuthin'. And then they went lookin' fer ranches."

Worn-out miners packed their tents and tools and bedrolls into wagons, added a trunk and a chest of drawers, cast-iron skillets, bacon, beans, and sacks of flour. Their wives tucked in the treasured family items: a china pitcher, a cut-glass bowl, a mirror, or a violin. Together, they hitched their team of horses to the wagon, tied the family cow behind it, gathered up their children, whistled for the family dog, and set out once more full of hopes and dreams.

They traveled slowly up the road that William Loveland had blasted over the Continental Divide in 1879, easing down its western side into the Blue River Valley. From there, they followed Tenmile Creek past walls of rugged cliffs, climbed an unnamed pass, and wound their way down into the Gore Creek Valley. They staked their tents, paced off the dimensions of cabins, and grubbed out stones for cabin foundations. At dusk, the women stirred up dough for biscuits and heated beans and coffee over the campfire. Weary from the day's work, the pioneers talked and dreamed of the good times ahead.

But it was one thing to explore the high country during the green and glorious days of summer and quite another to stay there all year. When autumn rains turned into snow on the high peaks, the surveyors had packed their gear and gotten out. So had the Utes. No one in his right mind stayed in the mountains after the snow started.

But the homesteaders chose to stay, to take what the country offered, to survive its challenges and dangers.

No man survived them better than Joseph Brett. A florist from the French province of Alsace-Lorraine, Brett emigrated to New York in 1876, made his way to Denver, heard about the mining furor in Leadville, and went there to see it. In 1878, he traveled north out of Leadville and followed the westward bend of the Eagle River to where it widened into pools at Lake Creek. Brett hoped to find gold, but instead he discovered rich, well-watered soil for farming and a forest filled with game.

Brett returned the following year to build a hewn-log, sod-roofed cabin on a bluff above the river. He ordered seed from Denmark, framed hot beds for celery, lettuce, and radishes, planted potatoes and asparagus, and bordered his walls and fences with peonies and roses. He married Red Cliff school teacher Marie Guenon and brought her to the ranch. Within a few years, "The Frenchman's" became a rendezvous in

*P*age 32, pioneer Charlie Baldauf sports sheepskin chaps. Left, Joseph Brett's ranch at Lake Creek above the Eagle River. (Baldauf and Brett Collections Photos)

the wilderness.

Even the Utes, some of whom still wandered the area, visited the ranch. Brett, gazing downriver from his vantage point on the bluff, sometimes spotted the huge and slovenly Colorow, a renegade Ute chief, trotting towards him with a band of friends. While Brett liked Colorow, he knew him to be light-fingered and always stowed his guns and other valuables in a hole under the kitchen floor before Colorow rode in. Marie heated coffee, rolled out dough for biscuits, and put a pot of jam on the table. The Indians spread the jam lavishly, gulped quarts of coffee, danced in the yard to shake it down, and came back for more.

Skilled with plow and gun, Joseph Brett prospered at his ranch on Lake Creek. And then, in February, 1884, he made a terrible mistake.

Early one morning, he and his friends left for a hunting trip in the country north of the ranch. They made their way down the bluff to cross the ice on the wide, shallow ponds of the Eagle River. Suddenly, the ice broke and Brett fell through, soaking his feet. Rather than go back for dry shoes, he continued the hunt. But later the temperature dropped sharply, and by the time Brett got back to the ranch his feet were nearly frozen. Desperate, he thrust his feet into the oven, but the sudden warmth did more harm than good. Within a few days, gangrene set in.

Brett's friends made him as comfortable as they could on a hand sled and pulled him 20 miles up river to Red Cliff. Four men anesthetized him with whiskey and held him down while doctors cut off both feet across the instep. In the casual manner of the day, they threw the amputated parts out the window. Brett, eyes glazed by pain and alcohol, later saw dogs carrying his feet around.

Brett spent weeks recovering. In April, a Red Cliff gossip column noted brightly his return to the ranch: "He is now entirely recovered and in almost as good condition as he was before his feet were made shorter." With hoof-shaped leather shoes made to accommodate his smaller feet, he learned to walk with two canes but found it easier to get around on his knees, padded with strips of burlap.

Despite his injury, Brett turned his wilderness ranch into a popular resort. The tracks of the Denver and Rio Grande Railroad came past the ranch in 1887, bringing wealthy Leadville businessmen to "The Frenchman's" for leisurely vacations. Brett set up two tents, one for sleeping and one for card-playing. When his bearded, bow-tied guests arrived, he hoisted the American flag, opened the liquor chest, and shuffled the cards.

Between bouts of heavy betting, the businessmen stood at the river waving split-bamboo fly rods over the riffles. Marie and daughter Louise laid out lavish dinners, one of which included beavertail soup, trout, fried elk steaks, venison loaf, frog saddles, and French salad.

Joseph Brett took the best and the worst that nature dealt and played

*J*oseph Brett, left, and the Brett house on
Lake Creek, above, with sporting
vacationers. Brett and his wife Marie
stand at the doorway with children
George and Louise. (Brett Collection)

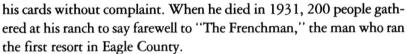

his cards without complaint. When he died in 1931, 200 people gathered at his ranch to say farewell to "The Frenchman," the man who ran the first resort in Eagle County.

In 1884, in Georgetown, Colorado, John Wesley Phillips, who had made his living as a teamster for the mines, decided to try ranching, a decision not made lightly for a man with seven children.

When his first wife died, John hired 15-year-old Mary Elnora Avery to care for his children. Although twice her age, he later married her. Mary's family was furious; on the wedding night her brothers pounded at the door to rescue her. "You'd better go away," shouted Phillips, "she's my wife now!"

John and Mary, with their seven children and the usual collection of horses, cows, chickens, dogs, and household goods, arrived at the high east end of the Gore Creek Valley in the summer of 1884. Once settled in a cabin there, Mary delivered babies regularly, seven of them, making a total of 14 young bodies to feed, clothe, and care for.

A proud woman, she accepted hand-me-downs from her Gore Creek neighbors but carefully took apart each dress and shirt, washed and pressed the pieces, and cut new clothes from her own patterns. Each spring she dosed her children with tonics of wild sage tea and onion syrup and sent them, scrubbed and neatly dressed, to the sod-roofed schoolhouse at a neighboring ranch. School was in session only during the summer months; by autumn, Mary had the whole tribe on her hands again.

One fall, her husband found a bolt of flannel in Leadville at a price he couldn't resist and bought her fifty yards of it. Mary spent weeks at

Visitors to Brett's Frenchman's Resort, above, left, lounge outside his card-playing tent. Brett flew the American flag and insisted that English be spoken at his place, explaining that "We're in America now." Photograph, above, right, shows him wearing his special shoes as he poses with daughter Louise and son Jim. Dr. Gilpin, facing page, was the pioneering doctor of Red Cliff who amputated portions of Joseph Brett's frozen feet. (Photos from Brett Collection and Red Cliff Museum)

A typical catch of the day, preceding page, at The Frenchman's Ranch in the early 1900s. The car was not so much a means of fishing access in that roadless era as a service to the crippled visitor whose crutches rest against its stern. Rules for guests at The Frenchman's included "No rowdiness, no hot water, wash up at the trough," facing page, top. The clientele normally excluded ladies; these, facing page, bottom, were probably family guests. Trapshooting, left, was a popular warmup for the sportsmen, who came primarily from Leadville. But the chief attraction was Eagle River fishing, below. Joseph Brett, host, stands third from right. (Brett Collection Photos)

Turn of the century riders follow the trail past Black Lake over what would become Vail Pass. (Baldauf Collection)

her sewing machine turning out nighties, slips, shirts, skirts, and rompers — all in black and red plaid. At least, she sighed, she could pick out her children easily against the snow.

John Wesley Phillips supplied mining towns with such delicious spring lamb and Irish potatoes that people in Red Cliff gathered quickly around his wagon when it rolled into town. He brought deer, elk, bear, grouse, and rabbit to his own family table and during the winter trapped wolves, foxes, marten, mink and beavers. When someone warned him about a law against killing beavers, he said: "It isn't God's law. They're on my place and they do a lot of damage and I'm goin' to trap 'em."

A stern disciplinarian, Phillips never allowed his daughters alone in a room with their boyfriends. And when he found his sons with a deck of cards, he threw the cards in the fire. "That's the way boys get to gambling, playing cards at home," he said.

Instead, he taught them how to make skis out of barnwood. They planed and sanded the boards and softened the ends in boiling water so they could bend the tips up. The boys nailed on leather straps for bindings, rubbed the bottoms with goose oil, and took their skis to the top of the pass for a three-mile downhill run back to the ranch.

For his own pleasure, Phillips hunted bears. "Up on Gore Creek, J.W. Phillips found bear sign one morning last week," reported the *Eagle County Times* in June, 1900. "Taking his rifle, he started on the trail, which after a while gave evidence of more than one bear. Coming to a down-timber patch, where great pines lay crossed and twined, J.W. mounted a huge, dead pine log for observation. Just as he got up, a bear

Visiting in the home of one of their many children, John Wesley Phillips and wife Mary Elnora reflect both the hardship and the romance of life on Gore Creek during its pioneer era. (Rockwood/Hammer Collection)

mounted the other end and started for him, and immediately another. To the right, a big cinnamon bear poked his nose through the willows that fringed the timber, and two smaller ones hopped out into the open.

"With two well directed shots, Mr. Phillips dropped the two bears on the log and then started after the other three, who, scared by the shots, had started for the hills. He finally located them in a sort of natural corral where he can go back and get them. J.W. returned to his undertaking duties and had bear steak for breakfast. Bruin had best hide out when Phillips takes to the warpath."

Phillips' daughter Rhoda worshipped her father and treasured her years with him on Gore Creek. "My Dad, he was a good provider," she said. "If he hadn't of been, we'd of starved to death. And I think — boy, he had courage, takin' a big family like that into the hills and makin' a go of it!"

By the early 1900s, homesteaders had settled most of the valley, their ranches linked by the winding path of Gore Creek and a single dirt road. At the west end, the road squeezed through a canyon so narrow that two wagons could not pass each other in that spot. Often, during winter and spring, deep snow closed the road for weeks.

At his ranch at the east end of the valley, Walt Mann rose at 4 a.m. each morning, sawed chunks of ice out of his ice pond, loaded his wagon, and creaked down the valley at dawn on his way to Minturn. His team of horses pulled him home late in the afternoon, with Mann nodding over the reins. "Watch out for Walt," his neighbors warned. "If he's asleep, his team will run you off the road."

Mann talked Charlie Baldauf, a miner from Gilman, into home-

*P*art of the Phillips clan, above, left, fishing at Black Lake, and Rhoda Phillips, above, right, at her pioneer home in what is now East Vail. (Rockwood/Hammer Collection) The Baldauf cabin, facing page, top, at Booth Creek still stands today, renovated and used by the Vail Mountain School. The Baldauf family, bottom, with Mary Baldauf standing at left, daughter Edna, seated at left, and Charlie at right. (Baldauf Collection)

steading in the valley. Charlie's wife, Mary, hoped to move to Glenwood Springs to get out of the snow, but Charlie, an ardent fly fisherman, preferred Gore Creek. In 1906, he used his hardrock mining know-how to blast rocks and willow shrubs and clear a spot for a cabin at the mouth of Booth Creek. When Mary and the children, Edna and John, moved in, they invited their Gore Creek neighbors for a Fourth of July picnic. That night they lit the sky over the valley with $10 worth of fireworks, "and in those days," said Edna, "you really got fireworks for $10."

Summer passed much too quickly. The homesteaders hurried to get their work done while the good weather lasted. One morning in September, a pale lace of snow appeared on the rocky heights of the Gore Range. The snow melted in a day or two, but a week later it fell again and did not melt. Summer gave way to a breezy, golden autumn. As the storms increased, the snow line descended the ridges above the cabins. Then one morning all the valley turned white.

The pace quickened. Women stirred at steaming kettles, pickling and preserving food for the winter. Men spent hours splitting and stacking firewood. The days shortened; lantern light winked over the evening meals.

Forced inside by cold and snow, the homesteaders pulled out treasured family books, woodworking projects, and games to play by the fireplace. The women sewed. "They was always buyin' yard goods and makin' clothes," said pioneer Charlie King. "Or tearin' up old clothes and makin' quilts. Patchwork quilts. Always."

When the snow deepened, timbering began on the mountain. Loggers sawed through the tree trunks at snow level, leaving six-foot stumps in a heavy snow year. Teams of horses pulled the trees down the slopes on sled-bobs.

Still dreaming of gold, a few ranchers whiled away long winter hours prospecting in the rocky cliffs behind their cabins. "Jake Ruder and Dave Evans are developing a nice quiet mining claim just this side of the Ruder ranch," reported a local newspaper. That claim produced more hope than gold.

Charlie Baldauf kept the valley road open with an A-drag, a primitive snowplow made of a heavy wooden frame that his team pulled through the snow to pack it down. Some winters the packed road ran level with the tops of the fences.

Deep snow or not, the homesteaders never missed a party. "The Gore Creek folks generally turn out strong for the dances," reported the *Eagle County Times* during the winter of 1900. "Last Monday night there was a musicale at the Shivelys that lasted until the early morning hours. Thursday of the same week, Walt Mann's house was invaded by neighbors for music and drama, after which Mrs. Mann spread an elegant oyster supper, then the floor was cleared and dancing indulged in for several hours. There's nothing but health and good spirits up on the Gore — and a world of hospitality."

The pioneers shared bad times, too. Death seemed especially sad in the darkness and cold of winter when the ground often froze too hard for burials. One April, Eliza Shively's niece died in childbirth near the Brett Ranch at Lake Creek. "At that time my grandmother Eliza lived on Gore Crik," said Charles King. "And she went down there on snowshoes. She walked 14 miles on snowshoes when they buried the girl and her baby."

In May, mothers peered out of cabin windows at the falling snow, spread mustard plasters on the chests of coughing children, and dreamed of warmer places. Rows of canned goods shrank on pantry shelves and piles of firewood dwindled. Still it snowed. On May 15, 1907, men cleared five feet of snow from the road at the west end of the valley. When supplies ran low, Gore Creek pioneers showed up at larger ranches along the Eagle River and offered to clean irrigation ditches in return for a sack of potatoes or a "shirtful of hay."

One spring, Charlie King's father had to return to work in the mines and left his wife alone at the ranch with their children. "We had this pond with big red cutthroat fish in it and my mother had an old 30-30 Winchester rifle," said Charlie. "If the fish wouldn't bite, she'd walk around the edges until she located a school of them fish, and then she'd blast in there with that rifle and they'd belly up, and we'd have fish for supper."

By the end of May, the last of the snow melted, "and then it was mud to the axles," declared Edna Baldauf. But the mud finally dried, and springtime warmth seeped into the valley.

In the 1920s, Colorado farmers found that lettuce grew deliciously firm and crisp at elevations above 7,000 feet. For a few years, a kind of happy insanity raged in remote valleys like Gore Creek as farmers found that lettuce-growing actually put money in their pockets. But deer frequently ravaged the lettuce fields, and farmers knew little about soil treatment or crop rotation.

"Then the market got tight," said Dick Hammer, whose family owned a ranch in the valley. "The people got picky and too much lettuce had to be culled. Down at the lettuce sheds, I saw piles of lettuce that they threw out. Piles of it. Nelson's cows used to go down there and eat

Facing page, the David Shively homestead, circa 1890, on the north side of the Gore Creek Valley, just east of the site of Vail, and Eliza Shively with grandson Frank Evans inside the house. (King Collection)

it. Those Gore Creek people made so much money, so quick, so easy, on lettuce. But it was a false prosperity."

The Depression ended prosperity, false and otherwise. Some hung on, and some sold out. Edna Baldauf sold 120 acres of her Booth Creek property for a total of $275.

The Katsos and the Kiahtipeses, Greek sheepmen, purchased valley ranches in the 1930s. Like the Utes, the sheepmen moved with the seasons. During the summer, their sheep grazed on Forest Service land in the high valleys above Gore Creek. In the fall, herders moved the animals down valley to the railroad and shipped them to Utah for winter graze. In the spring, the sheep moved slowly up the valley while the lambs were born.

One summer, when a mountain lion developed a taste for Gore Valley lamb, one of the herders built a brush corral under a big pine tree and put several lambs in the corral, hoping to lure the lion in and shoot it. Humming happily to himself, he climbed the tree to begin his vigil. A slight sound made him look up. In the branches above sat the lion, curiously attentive. The herder fell out of the tree and broke his shoulder, and the local ranger drove him, no longer humming, to the doctor in Minturn.

Sheep still drifted up and down Gore Creek when latter-day pioneers Frank and Marge Haas, lured by the romance of high country ranching, bought 520 acres on Red Sandstone Creek.

*P*ages 52 and 53, Don and Arlo Kellog hauling logs in the Gore Creek Valley in 1938. Kellogs and relatives, right, gather at their home sawmill. The Kellog ranch at Red Sandstone Creek, bottom right, was later purchased by Frank and Marge Haas. (Kellog Collection Photos) In a 1940s photo, bottom left, sheep crowd the present location of the Safeway store in West Vail. The Gore Creek Schoolhouse, now a museum at Ford Park, stands in the background. (Kiahtipes Collection)

They moved into the ranchhouse during a heavy snowstorm in April. The place smelled awful. Resident packrats had insulated the walls for years with pea pods, oats, and rat droppings. Marge scraped out bushels of the stuff, but the smell hung on for months. Their only water ran from a spring outside. Wintertime trips to the outhouse were so uncomfortable that Marge's father lined the seat with fur.

Frank had his dream ranch but no money, no credit, and no stock animals. He went to work as a logger while Marge raised rabbits, and they put aside every possible cent until they saved enough to buy a few cows.

After World War II began, the Army built Camp Hale in the Pando Valley, 23 miles south of Gore Creek. Troopers from the 10th Mountain Division often drove through the valley on their way to Denver and stopped at the Haas' for one of Marge's home-cooked meals. Frank and Marge, in return, visited their new friends at the camp. On one trip, Frank noted the mountain of garbage that 14,000 troopers produced. Not one to pass up something for nothing, he made arrangements to bring portions of it home. He then invested in some pigs and successfully raised them on Camp Hale garbage.

Marge Haas loved the Gore Creek summers. She said it was worth getting through the winters just to see the snow melt and the valley green up. But in the spring of 1950, after it snowed for 40 days in a row, Marge had enough. "Let's get out of here, Frank," she said. "This place isn't good for anything except a bunch of skiers."

THE BIRTH

OF A

SKI RESORT

◆

III

PETER SEIBERT, a 10th mountain division ski trooper from Camp Hale, Colorado, nearly lost his life in the Appenine Mountains of northern Italy during World War II. On Monte Terminale, a mortar shell ripped his body from foot to face. Doctors doubted that he would walk again. Skiing? Out of the question.

"He came home from the war with his face and arm and leg half blown away — barely walking," said a friend. "The survivors were in Aspen, so Pete and his friend, Morrie Shepard, went to Aspen. That was in 1946. Pete would hook that bad leg behind the knee of his good leg and he'd ski that way. By 1947, he was racing. He was a war hero, a racer with a Purple Heart and a Bronze Star. There was a romance to him — everybody wanted to know Pete. He could open doors and sit down with corporate leaders."

Earl Eaton met Peter Seibert at Aspen after the war. Eaton, born in a homesteader's cabin a few miles west of the Gore Creek Valley, grew up on skis and had helped build Camp Hale for the ski troopers.

Seibert and Eaton not only shared a passion for skiing but a dream of building their own resort. "Everybody in Aspen would talk about going out and finding a ski area," said Eaton. "The ski instructors and the ski bums — everybody had big ideas."

It was during that time that Americans fell in love with skiing. The 10th Mountain Division ski troopers brought glory and romance to the sport, *apres-ski* added the spice of social adventure, and fashion replaced the skier's lumpy, woolen look with sleek, slim, stretch pants. Skiing boomed, bringing smiles to travel agencies and retailers. The Colorado tourist bureau called skiing an "industry without a smokestack."

Investors, however, steered clear of the ski resort business. Only a few resorts in the country were making any money at that time, and it took plenty of money to satisfy the new breed of skier. Gone were the stalwart, knickered pioneers who shouldered wooden skis and trudged to the mountaintop for one exhilarating run through trees and crusted snow. Post-war skiers wanted more than just a run for their money. They wanted fast lifts, groomed snow, and if needed, the services of the ski patrol. They expected hot chili at noon, a dry martini *apres-ski,* béarnaise on the filet, a hot shower, and clean sheets.

Even when profitable, the ski season was short, skiers were fickle, and the snowfall unreliable. Resorts around the country were in enough financial hot water to melt the snow on their slopes.

Still, developers traipsed through valleys all over Colorado with plans to cut down chunks of pristine forest, scrape off meadows, throw bridges over crystal streams, and bring on multitudes in ski boots. But how many ski areas did Colorado need? Who would be responsible if the developer ran out of money and left weedy parking lots and skeletal lift towers among the lodgepole pines?

*P*eter Seibert

That dilemma put the squeeze on the United States Forest Service, which administered much of Colorado's mountain land. Requests for permits to use that land for skiing poured into Forest Service offices, raising venerable questions about preservation and proper land use.

Squarely in the crossfire between developers and conservationists stood forester Paul Hauk, Colorado native, life-long skier, avalanche expert, and all-around mountain man. Hauk's influence on the ski industry was one to be reckoned with. When he retired in 1977, *The Denver Post* Ski Editor Charlie Meyers wrote: "It is very likely that Paul Hauk has exercised more leverage over the direction of skiing on public lands than any other Forest Service official. Whenever there was a ski decision to be made, Hauk's smoke-gray crewcut always was among the group with heads and voices lowered in consultation."

During the ski boom, Paul Hauk rode into action on the side of slow and cautious growth. He had just moved to Glenwood Springs in the summer of 1957 when yet another request for a ski area permit came in. Peter Seibert and Earl Eaton, it seemed, had found their mountain.

It was not much of a mountain by Colorado standards. No one had even bothered to give it a name. Historian Marshall Sprague, writing later for *The New York Times,* described it as "a placid, oblong pile, nicely clad in aspen, spruce, and lodgepole pine."

The mountain slanted to the south out of the Gore Creek Valley in a way that made it impossible to see what was on top, which is why Seibert and Eaton and other people interested in potential ski areas had driven past the base of it innumerable times without a second glance.

But Eaton, prospecting for uranium just 15 miles from where he grew up, suddenly recognized the mountain's possibilities and told Seibert about it. Both men, at that time, were working at Loveland Basin ski area. In March, 1957, they strapped on skis and after climbing through deep snow for seven hours, crested the summit of what would become known as Vail Mountain.

To the south lay steep, open bowls, backed by the dramatic profile of the Mount of the Holy Cross; to the north, slopes varied enough in length and pitch to satisfy every kind of skier. The summit, below timberline and sheltered from wind, stood 3,050 vertical feet above the Gore Creek Valley. And beyond the valley rose the stunning pinnacles

Camp Hale, where the Tenth Mountain Division trained during World War II. Many troopers fell in love with the Colorado high country during that period and returned later to take an active part in the development of Colorado ski resorts. (Photos Courtesy of Colorado Ski Museum)

Earl Eaton paints a model of Vail and Beaver Creek mountains. (Photo by David Lokey)

of the Gore Range, propped like an elegant theater-set against the sky.

"The first time I stood on top," said Seibert, "I knew it was as good as any ski mountain I'd seen."

When Paul Hauk inspected the mountain in late August, he agreed. "It has far greater potential and variety than Aspen," he wrote in a Forest Service report. "Snow conditions should be better than Aspen, due to the slightly higher elevations, colder local temperatures, and better exposures.

"My impression, from talking to Seibert and Eaton," he concluded, "is that if necessary land can be purchased or leased with option to buy at anywhere near a reasonable price, we will have another formal application on our hands. The area has quite a potential, and I would venture to say that Seibert might even resign his job and promote the financial backing which for him, with all his contacts, would not be too difficult."

Sure enough, Seibert contacted Bob Fowler, a Denver attorney he had met at Aspen. Fowler drove up to look at the mountain, the valley, and the development possibilities. He liked them all. So did John Conway, a Denver real estate appraiser.

Seibert and Eaton had their mountain, but they needed land at its base, where the Forest Service required food, housing, and parking facilities for skiers. They had to buy that land quietly; news of ski development would send prices skyrocketing. Therefore, they created the Transmontane Rod and Gun Club, its rustic name suggesting a few good fellows who wanted nothing but a little hunting lodge and some land along a trout stream like Gore Creek. Charter members: Peter Seibert, Earl Eaton, Bob Fowler, and John Conway.

With quiet persistence, John Conway acquired the land. "Conway could talk to the farmers for hours," said Seibert. "It would have driven me crazy. But he'd stop every couple of months and visit them. They'd stand around and kick tractor tires and spit at beetles and pretty soon they got on a first name basis. After a while they decided to sell."

Gore Creek rancher John Hanson sold first. His 520-acre ranch, once owned by Frank and Marge Haas, became the future site of Vail Village. Hanson sold the land for $110 an acre.

Early in 1959, two more of Seibert's Aspen friends joined The Transmontane Rod and Gun Club. But attorney Jack Tweedy and oilman George Caulkins, both from Denver, were skeptical at first. "Peter, is this a hobby or a business?" asked Tweedy. "My friends suggested I keep my house at Aspen in case Vail didn't work out," said Caulkins.

On May 11, 1959, Seibert and Eaton applied to the Forest Service for a permit for year-round recreational development on Vail Mountain. The next day Paul Hauk turned them down.

"We agree that Vail is feasible," explained Hauk, "and has the

required potential for another major development on the White River National Forest. However, since we have never given you any encouragement regarding a permit, we are disapproving your application. The reasons are: 1) There is no real public need for the development at this time. 2) We have an obligation to existing area permittees, especially at Aspen, who are entitled to complete their development and be allowed to 'get into the black' before new areas are permitted on this forest.

"Our primary obligation is to Whip Jones at Aspen Highlands. We estimate that he will need until 1965 to show a net profit at his ski area. At that time, we will be happy to reconsider your application for a permit depending on forest and state-wide needs. You, of course, have the right to appeal our decision."

Attorneys Fowler and Tweedy appealed immediately. The Forest Supervisor, Hauk's boss, denied their appeal and the battle lines were drawn.

Seibert produced statistics proving the need for new ski areas; Hauk provided statistics to prove the opposite. Eventually, the shoot-out moved to Washington, D.C., where Colorado congressmen pondered whether the Forest Service should indeed guarantee the financial success of one ski area before another began. Phone calls and documents crisscrossed the country throughout the summer. In September, the Forest Service relented and approved the permit.

The permit carried strict conditions, however, requiring that money for trails, lift facilities, and the first year's operating expenses — estimated at a total of $1.8 million — be on hand by December, 1961. Clearly, the time had come for the Rod and Gun club to go after big game.

Fortunately, Seibert's friends knew where to find it. Phones rang in the homes of corporate executives, and on golf courses the discussion turned to the remote Colorado mountain and its interesting possibilities. The search centered on those in the 70 percent tax bracket who

*P*roperty purchased by the Transmontane Rod and Gun Club as seen from the bottom of Vail Mountain. Plume of smoke comes from sawmill on Red Sandstone Creek. Other than land, the Vail Corporation's sole assets in 1960 consisted of a tin-roofed hut on the mountaintop and a Kristi Kat. Below, Bob Fowler and his wife Ann stand at the hut while Earl Eaton shovels snow off the roof. (Vail Associates Photos)

could write off losses without losing any sleep.

"We told them they were bell cows," said Seibert, "and that we came to them because we were sure they could afford to lose money. If the thing went belly-up, they weren't going to get anything. I guess they thought that was pretty up-front, so they went along with it."

By December, 1959, 21 men from nine states had taken a chance on Peter Seibert's dream by investing $5,000 each in the Vail Corporation. The Transmontane Rod and Gun Club, where neither shot was fired nor lure cast, was put to rest.

The Vail Corporation bought the Katsos ranch for $75,000, adding another 500 acres to its valley property. It put Seibert and Eaton on the payroll, hired an architect to design the village, sought advice on water, soil, roads and bridges, and made a silent movie illustrating the wonderful skiing on Vail Mountain. Money ran dangerously low and so did the permit's alloted time.

*P*eter Seibert tours Vail Mountain on the Kristi Kat. (Vail Associates Photo)

In 1960 came the disquieting news of a new ski area at Breckenridge, solidly financed and 30 miles closer to Denver skiers. At that time, the sole assets of the Vail Corporation, other than land, consisted of a jeep, a tin-roofed hut and outhouse on the mountaintop, and a little red over-the-snow vehicle called the Kristi Kat.

The corporation members also found themselves in the cow business. With everything up in the air financially, they felt it important to keep intact the valuable Forest Service grazing privileges that went with their ranch properties in case they had to sell them. Since grazing privileges had to be used to remain valid, the Vail Corporation bought 50 cows and hired a cowboy to ride herd.

Meanwhile, George Caulkins prowled the concrete canyons of New York City looking for underwriters to fund the project. "They were all very polite," he said. "The top underwriters sent me on to the grade B underwriters, and those people sent me on to firms I'd never even heard of. Finally, I realized that no one in New York was going to touch this pie-in-the-sky in Colorado."

In March, 1961, Seibert asked the Forest Service to reduce the cash-on-hand requirement. Paul Hauk didn't budge. "Vail appears to be following the typical ski area promotion pattern," he wrote. "First the big 'snow job' with detailed planning, promotion brochures, movies, etc.; then the inevitable paring down when the cash isn't available."

Tweedy and Fowler pondered the money problems and considered selling limited partnerships in the venture. Caulkins had put together deals like that in the oil business; the idea might work for Vail. One hundred limited partnerships at $10,000 each, plus a loan from a bank, would bring in the $1.8 million they needed by December. They could throw in four lifetime ski passes per buyer for good measure. Caulkins said he'd give it a try.

How Vail Got Its Name

Vail owes its name to a few angry vigilantes who operated in the railroad town of Salida, Colorado, back in 1939.

Charles D. Vail, then chief engineer for the highway department, had paved hundreds of miles through the Colorado mountains and had made plans to improve and reroute a road over Monarch Pass in the mountains west of Salida. Local residents preferred a route over Marshall Pass southwest of town, but Charles Vail put the pass where he wanted it.

The folks in Salida then declared that they should at least be allowed to name the pass; since the highway followed Agate Creek, they chose the name Monarch-Agate Pass. No sooner had they made that decision than signs reading VAIL PASS appeared along the route.

Salida was in a furor. The chamber of commerce sent a letter of protest to Governor Ralph Carr. Local vigilantes splashed black paint on the offending signs and simply painted out the "P" on one of them. Governor Carr ended the fracas by officially designating the route Monarch Pass.

That satisfied Salida but left the highway department looking for a pass to label Vail. They found one in an isolated spot west of the Tenmile Range, one known to locals as Black Gore Pass. When Black Gore Pass became Vail Pass, a county newspaper commented: "We see no objection to this. The pass is without a name, and Vail Pass is just as good as any."

Actually, the pass had been named a half-century earlier by Theodore Dru Alison Cockerell, a young English naturalist who immigrated to Colorado in 1887 hoping to heal his consumptive lungs.

Cockerell camped on the pass in September, 1888, found arrowheads and fragments of pottery, surmised the place to be an ancient camping ground, and named it Pottery Pass. When work began on Interstate 70, archeologists for the highway department rediscovered and excavated the site and confirmed Cockerell's findings.

As for the name of the future Vail, a forester first referred to it in 1957 as the Mill Creek-Two Elk Creek area; others called it the Vail Pass area. A Vail Corporation member wanted to use the Ute name — The Shining Mountains — but Peter Seibert scratched that idea. "When mountains shine, it means they're icy," he said.

Vail it was. Short, easy, euphonious.

Thanks, Salida. ■

He and Seibert crammed suitcases, a movie projector, and the Vail ski film into George's Porsche. "I can't tell you how many thousands of miles we covered," said Caulkins. "It wasn't like raising money for oil wells. Putting together a ski area as a money-raising proposition had never been done before. If we hadn't had a lot of good friends who came in on a questionable investment based on friendship, I wouldn't have been able to do it."

The Caulkins-Seibert road show turned up in homes, clubs, board rooms, motels, the Mayo Clinic, and a tugboat in the Providence, Rhode Island, harbor. They showed the Vail ski movie four or five times a day. The film tore, projector bulbs burned out, and the audience fell asleep. George got sick of repeating the sales pitch over and over. Peter sometimes stole away to a nearby golf course. Avid skiers attended the talks in Milwaukee, Minneapolis, St. Paul, Chicago, and Kalamazoo, but no one bought.

George finally sold the first partnership unit to a cousin in Detroit. He immediately got on the phone to potential buyers in cities they had already visited and told them the units were selling like hot cakes.

Actually, they sold only 38 out of the 100 by mid-summer. With time running out, Caulkins went to five wealthy Vail Corporation members and promised that if they each underwrote five partnerships, he would underwrite the last ten. They agreed. "That was the thing that put it over the top," said Caulkins, "because word got out that it was a *fait accompli* and the people started coming in."

While driving through Texas in August, Caulkins and Seibert dreamed up another sales pitch. Along with the four lifetime lift passes, why not offer a Vail homesite as part of the package? "People in Texas did not understand the value of lift passes, but they sure understood the value of land," said George. Sales picked up immediately.

Skiers bought 50 percent of the partnerships; others signed up simply for the romance of skiing or because of the considerable charms of George Caulkins and Peter Seibert. As for Caulkins, he knew one thing for sure: no one expected to make any money out of Vail.

With financing assured and the permit in the bag, the Vail Corporation threw an announcement party. Coloradans read the news on December 28, 1961:

> The nation's largest ski area will be built on the west side of Vail Pass, The Denver Post learned Thursday . . . Major facilities will include a 9,500 foot Bell gondola with 63 four-passenger cabins, two mile-long chair lifts and a 1,000 foot beginners' lift . . . Peter Seibert, a former Aspen ski instructor and former manager of Loveland Ski Basin, will be general manager of the area.

With opening date set for December 15, 1962, Seibert, relentlessly cheerful, took on the formidable task of building lifts, trails, and all the base facilities in less than a year.

First, he went after more help. As his assistant manager and publicity director, he hired Bob Parker, the former editor of *Skiing Magazine*. Seibert then went to Aspen and convinced boyhood friend Morrie Shepard to head the Vail Ski School. Shepard, in turn, hired Aspen ski instructor Rod Slifer as his assistant.

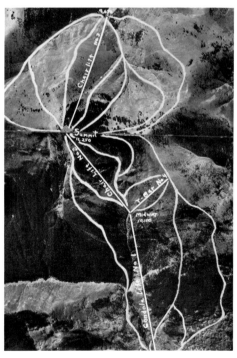

*M*id-Vail, top, as it looked when Pete Seibert and Earl Eaton first discovered Vail Mountain. An aerial photograph showed potential investors the proposed lift and trail construction, above. Lift number 4, the T-Bar, was never built. (Vail Associates Photos)

*E*arl Eaton aligns a lift tower, above. (Vail Associates Photo) Facing page, construction of Vail Village and mountain trails in the summer of 1962. Trailers, parked near the village site, served as employee housing. Workers used aspen logs to stabilize re-bar when concrete was poured for gondola tower foundations. At Mid-Vail, stacked chairs awaited installation, and lack of snow provided easy access to the gondola terminal by car. (Photos by Ted Bischoff)

Hiring assistants was one thing, but finding a place for them to live quite another. There was only one house in Vail, a chalet built in 1961 by corporation members Fitzhugh and Eileen Scott as an act of faith in the project. Across the valley, Earl Eaton and his family had moved into the old farmhouse at Red Sandstone Creek. With those two exceptions, there was no housing in the valley at all.

To ease the problem, Seibert moved four house trailers into the willows along Gore Creek. The Scotts opened part of their house for office space and shared a priceless luxury — the only bathroom in Vail. The project's single phone was a four-party line, best used after 10 p.m. when the lines were clear.

Minturn, six miles west, supplied minimal housing and such amenities as a grocery store, a hardware store, and a couple of bars. "Night life was exciting," said Slifer. "We'd drive to Minturn for a six-pack. Then we'd sit around drinking beer and naming ski runs."

It snowed heavily during the spring of 1962, and when the snow melted in the spring, the local forest ranger refused to allow any work on the mountain until the ground dried. Construction work turned the village site into a quagmire, so infuriating a rancher whose property lay immediately to the east that he staked a sign reading: STAY OUT! ANYONE COMING IN HERE WILL BE SHOT TO HELL! "We had the place so torn up he must have thought he'd been run over by a bulldozer," said Seibert.

One day, he and Rod Slifer visited the rancher. "He was mad because somebody had blocked his irrigation ditch," said Slifer. "We drove into the yard, and Peter told me I'd better stay in the car. He knocked on the door and the guy greeted him with what looked like a cannon in his hand. He chased us off the property and said he was going to shoot the next guy that came on his land and that we better get his ditch fixed."

The Forest Service permit stipulated lodging for at least 150, but the Vail Corporation, still scraping bottom financially, had no funds to build a lodge. Hotel chains sniffed disdainfully when offered the chance to build in Vail. They had never heard of the place. Fortunately, George Caulkins' partner, Harley Higbie, pieced together another limited partnership to finance The Lodge at Vail.

But Seibert feared The Lodge might not be done in time. As a backup, he offered a motel site near the highway to Ray Hankamer of Houston. He also offered a franchise for a gas station, its exclusivity guaranteed until the station pumped 600,000 gallons of gas a year.

Hankamer offered that franchise to several oil companies in return for their underwriting the cost of a motel, but most refused. Gulf Oil Corporation wrote: "We doubt that enough business can be generated from your customers alone, and we have no knowledge and can think of no resort where a service station is supported from the people who come to take advantage of its sports offerings."

The Continental Oil Company, however, swallowed the bait, underwrote the building of the Vail Village Inn, and placed its gas station on what became an Interstate 70 interchange.

As the summer of 1962 rolled around, a steady stream of suppliers chugged over the narrow Vail Pass road, and the ripsaw screech and hammerblow of construction in the sheep pasture rose to fever pitch. Seibert, the visionary, served as corporate chief, construction manager,

and consummate cheerleader. Every hour of every day another decision had to be made. Seibert made them quickly. "If something had to go someplace, we just went ahead and put it there," he said. "There wasn't time to study anything."

One day in August, Bob Parker, looking over requisition orders and work schedules, saw a terrible mistake in the making. The Bell gondola, the only lift out of the village, had to be ready and working by December 15. But gondola engineers in Lucerne, Switzerland, had set the completion date for the following February. When Parker called Lucerne to straighten things out, the Bell engineers politely informed him that the shipping arrangements had been made and nothing could be changed.

"I quickly developed an expertise in shipping matters," said Parker. "I located a transport expert in Brussels. I spent a lot of time on the phone in the middle of the night, talking to Europe. We intercepted gondola shipments, took them off barges or boats, put them on trucks, and got them to the airport in Brussels. We totally reorganized the shipping schedule, but we got everything here and the gondola built by December 15."

Summer ended, time ran short, and daily glitches and near-disasters kept the tension high. A workman buried the valve for the water line to the gas station, and a major dig took place to find it. One of the house trailers caught fire and burned like a torch, fortunately on a weekend when it was unoccupied. In October, a grass fire burned rapidly up the west slope of the mountain, just north of Minturn. Volunteers spent most of the day beating out the flames.

On the day of the fire, Earl Eaton and his crew finished stringing cable for the Back Bowls chair, clamped the cable, and used a tractor to put tension on it. The crew then relaxed, stetched out on the grass, and opened their lunch boxes. Suddenly, the clamps gave way and one mile of steel cable came alive. It snaked past the crew, whipped down the slope, wrapped itself around one of the huge support towers, yanked it out of its concrete foundation, and tossed it like a stick 200 yards down the hill. Incredibly, no one was hurt.

In November, amid the chaos, the two lodges neared completion. The Lodge at Vail rose stylishly in the village, replicating the time-honored Lodge at Sun Valley and boasting the managerial talents of Siegfried Faller Jr., who had spent his entire life at top European and American hotels and would oversee the French silverware, flaming dishes, and other elegant accoutrements at The Lodge.

At the Vail Village Inn, however, the first manager quit before the building was even finished, and Ray Hankamer hired Charles Gersbach, a Denver travel agent who knew nothing whatsoever about managing hotels. Gersbach flew to Galveston for a crash course in hotel management and then moved into a tiny house in Minturn with six other members of the Inn's staff. "Every day I would look up in a book to see how to run a hotel," he said. "Up front I could make it look like a hotel, but I had no clue as to how to do things like a night audit."

Hankamer also put Gersbach in charge of the Inn's restaurant and bar as well as the bus depot and gas station next door, hoping that Gersbach could keep the Inn's public image on the same high level as that of The Lodge. Gersbach did his best.

When General Motors provided The Lodge with a Buick station

The Lodge at Vail and the Vail Village Inn under construction during the fall of 1962. (Photos by Ted Bischoff)

wagon dubbed a "ski wagon," Ray Hankamer heard about it. "Charlie," he drawled over the phone, "y'all get me one of those Buicks." A week later the Vail Village Inn had its own ski wagon.

Hoping to match the posh Austrian flavor at The Lodge with a little European flair at the Vail Village Inn, Gersbach even produced a French chef. Seibert had hired a man named Ed Kilby, who lived in Minturn with his Indian wife, to cook for construction crews. Kilby, always with porkpie hat on his head, specialized in chicken-fried steak and other solid American grub. With construction jobs ending for the winter, Seibert feared he might lose him. He asked Gersbach to find Kilby a job. Gersbach smiled and shortly thereafter announced that French chef Pierre Kilbeaux had arrived to preside over the kitchen at the Vail Village Inn.

As opening day approached, the jobs piled up and everyone worked overtime, often at tasks they knew little or nothing about. Public relations man Bob Parker found himself designing the layout of gas pipes for the village. Oil executives George Caulkins and Harley Higbie installed the gas system and designed the water and sewer systems. Rod Slifer ran a one-man real estate department. Iron workers at The Lodge tied steel for the gondola towers at night. And Charlie Gersbach nearly went crazy keeping track of the Inn, the restaurant, the bar, the bus depot, and the chicken-fried talents of Pierre Kilbeaux.

Out on the highway, a small sign announced: VAIL, OPENING DECEMBER 1962. By the beginning of that month, it seemed unlikely. Marshall Sprague, writing for *The New York Times,* described the scene:

> It has been a long time, if ever, since anyone spent $5,000,000 in a few months to start a new ski resort. That is the situation here, and the result is an incredible frenzy of organized chaos, scattered over six square miles of what used to be a peaceful mountain wilderness.
>
> Today's seeming chaos at Vail is, of course, merely the appearance of modern technology applied to skiing — a far, far cry from 30 years ago when New England's pioneers started their resorts with a model-T engine and a few hundred feet of rope. Two hundred plumbers, electricians and the like reside at Vail now, mostly in trailers with many portable heated stoves, equipped with every kind of power tool. Huge transit-mix trucks climb the steep access road, mixing cement as they head for the 200 cubic foot anchorage of the upper gondola terminal. A tremendous crane waddled like a dinosaur up the road lately, followed by trucks from Denver loaded with concrete rafters, prestressed and cambered like a ski. In one day the crane lifted and placed the rafters to form the terminal's roof.

*V*ail's four-passenger gondola, initially the only lift out of the village, enters the terminal at Mid-Vail. (Vail Associates Photo) Below, Peter Seibert's dream comes true. (Photo by Peter Runyon)

Logo Longevity

V ail's logo, as familiar as its name and almost inseparable from it, owes its good looks and longevity to Dick Hauserman, formerly of Cleveland, Ohio, who served on the board of directors of the Vail Corporation.

At a meeting in Colorado in the summer of 1961, Peter Seibert showed Hauserman several proposed logo ideas for the new ski area. Hauserman did not like any of the sketches, which included snowflakes, pine cones, and crossed skis, symbols he thought had been used too often and that reminded him of eastern ski areas. Vail needed something new.

Hauserman returned to Cleveland and located Bob Wolaver, a draftsman who had a good reputation in the field of graphic design. The two men spent many evenings working on the logo. Gradually, the V for Vail evolved into a two-element design with a "blue-sky" V inverted over a "black mountain" V and the implied white line of snow running between.

Hauserman made a formal presentation of his logo to Vail Corporation board members. But by that time, many other ideas had been proposed, and opinions varied on which one to choose. Some thought Hauserman's design a little too "far out." Hauserman, however, believed in his logo and knew it was simply a question of getting people used to it.

At that time, when nothing had been built and Vail existed only in the minds of its founders, board members were plagued with the problem of explaining how to locate the ski area. Endlessly, they pointed out to friends and businessmen that Vail was halfway between Denver and Aspen or that it was two-thirds of the way from Denver to Glenwood Springs.

Hauserman turned that problem to good advantage. He made a map showing the road from Denver to Aspen and at the site of Vail he placed his logo. He printed the map on calling cards and distributed 100 cards to each board member.

His familiarization plan worked well. In due time, the logo became official, and with only slight modifications its clear, simple statement has been part of the Vail scene ever since. ■

Swiss engineers in tassled stocking caps check the lift towers, tilted perpendicular to the slope of the hill, instead of vertical, as of old. The towers came up to Vail from a Houston dock, dismantled like a toy construction set. Trucks are dumping spools of high tension wire and creosoted power poles. Linesmen, weighed down by tool vests, string wires for the 18 phones of the ski patrol.

With the pace so frantic, no one gave much thought to the weather, which remained clear and dry. As for opening day itself, some barely remembered it.

"The mood was not unlike the mood in wartime when you're going into combat," said Bob Parker. "The generals have decided the direction to go, the trucks are rolling, the commitment's been made, and you don't think about anything except getting on with it. That's the way it was here, opening day."

Looking back, Earl Eaton thought the skiing was free on the first day but wasn't sure. Charlie Gersbach recalled an opening day banquet at the Vail Village Inn when a pipe broke and poured water out of a ceiling fixture directly over the banquet table.

"Opening day," mused Rod Slifer. "I guess it just started, and we were all so busy there was no time to stop and congratulate each other. I don't even remember the date."

But George Caulkins remembered. He invested in a 3,000-acre citrus farm that year and talked several others into the same venture. While sunshine warmed the slopes of Vail, the temperature dropped to freezing in Florida and snow fell on the oranges.

Bob Parker did grab a few minutes that first day to see if anything was going on in the village. "There must have been skiers there," he said, "but what I saw first were some down-county folks in cowboy boots riding the gondola out of curiosity."

So Vail began with dust in its streets and the snow at its crest only ankle deep. Peter Seibert, who made all the right moves on the long road from dream to reality, had the last vital decision taken out of his hands. He could not make it snow.

It didn't matter. The congratulations, the speeches, the champagne, and the crowds came later.

So did the snow, bountifully as always. And as always, in its own good time.

*D*ecember 15, 1962, Vail's opening day, above, with no snow in the village. The lower photo shows Vail Mountain during its first season. Note the number of private homes already built at the base of the mountain on right. (Photos by Vail Associates)

FIRST

YEARS

IV

"THERE IS NO VAIL, COLORADO," said the Hertz representative at Denver's Stapleton Airport in January, 1963. "See?" she went on, unfolding a Colorado map. "There's Minturn, Avon, Eagle, and there's Glenwood Springs — you can drop the car off there. But there is no Vail."

Joe and Anne Staufer, formerly of the Elbow Beach Surf Club in Bermuda, knew there had to be a Vail out there somewhere because they had an interview scheduled with the ski resort operators. They rented the car and headed west into the mountains over the switchbacking loops of Loveland Pass, through the deep defile of Tenmile Canyon, and up the long eastern slope of Vail Pass. They noted the name of the pass with relief. Surely, Vail must be right around the bend.

But when they drove down the pass into the Gore Creek Valley, the narrow, two-lane road simply curved on to the west, and they had no choice but to follow it. Finally, they saw smoke curling from the chimney of an old cabin, a relic of the homestead days. "Do you know anything about a place called Vail?" they asked the man who came to the door. "Keep going that way," he answered, waving to the west.

At last, they found Vail. No wonder the woman at Stapleton had never heard of it. On the north side of the road stood the abandoned Gore Creek Ranger Station and on the south side a gas station and the squared buildings of the Vail Village Inn. Behind the Inn lay nothing but a stretch of snow-clogged willows, The Lodge at Vail, and a small cluster of buildings still under construction. A few houses among the trees at the base of the mountain completed the scene. For Joe and Anne Staufer, it was a long way and a far cry from the Elbow Beach Surf Club.

Yet the Staufers traded the warm sands of Bermuda for raw mountain living with good reason. A brand-new ski resort offered the perfect opportunity for hotel managers, shop keepers, chefs, and ski instructors looking for a change. Whether Vail would ever amount to anything more than a few good ski runs, no one knew. But it was worth a try, a chance to make it.

The investors who built homes at the base of the mountain did not seem worried about Vail's future. The corporate chiefs of such companies as Sears Roebuck, Upjohn, Bell Helicopter, Quaker Oats, and Schlitz — all of whom had far grander places to vacation than the Gore Creek Valley — astonished Vail founders by building houses that ran six figures in price.

A few of the wealthy settled as permanent residents of Vail. "I guess you could characterize them primarily as middle-aged dropouts from more civilized pursuits," said Bob Parker. "We had ex-bankers, ex-stockholders, ex-construction executives, ex-executives of major oil companies — men and women who were tired of the day-to-day grind in the big city and decided to seek another lifestyle."

*D*uring the resort's first years, the Vail
Village Inn, left, lay on the outskirts of
town. An oilman from Dallas, Texas,
built his Vail vacation home, above, in
the summer of 1963; Pepi Gramshammer
put up his lodge the following year.
(Photos by Vail Associates, upper left, the
Vail Trail, above, Gunther Hofler, left)

Clockwise from upper left: Early ski school form, the extraordinary Roger Staub, fashion during the 1960s, view from the top of Vail Mountain, and practicing a kick turn.

VAIL ASSOCIATES

BARRY STOTT

VAIL ASSOCIATES

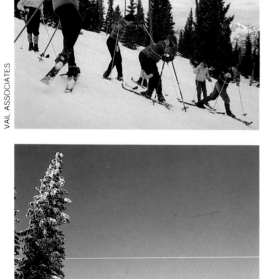

BARRY STOTT

BARRY STOTT

Clockwise from upper left: Perfect powder, early ski filming, Golden Peak with fall colors, the Vail Valley in 1965, and a spring skiing scene in 1963.

An early ski school brochure features director Morrie Shepard and an international cast of characters.

Morrie SHEPARD

Native New Englander, former asst. director Aspen Ski School. Chief Examiner, Rocky Mtn. Ski Instructors. Master of deep powder.

Pepi GRAMSHAMMER

From Innsbruck, Austria. Austrian National Team star. IPSRA professional. A great racer who can improve any skier's technique.

Roy PARKER

Lives in Georgetown, Colo. Former director Loveland Basin ski school. Skilled, patient instructor—the epitome of elegance in deep powder. Assistant school director.

Ricky ANDENMATTEN

Hails from Zermatt, Switzerland, where he was nationally certified instructor, mountain guide. Specializes in wedeln and parallel skiing.

Manfred SCHOEBER

Talented guide, mountain climber and ski teacher from Bavaria. Returns to Vail from expedition to Asia's Hindu Kush range. Leads top class in high speed skiing.

Rod SLIFER

Native Coloradan, former top instructor at Aspen, permanent resident of Vail. An experienced all around teacher who doubles as assistant school director.

EXPERTS—learn deep powder and wedeln on America's most challenging slopes.

INTERMEDIATES—improve your technique on Vail's wide, well-packed trails.

BEGINNERS—master the fundamentals in one day on Gopher Hill . . . then ride the gondola to exciting Swingsville.

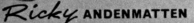

CERTIFIED INTERNATIONAL INSTRUCTORS TEACHING THE NEW AMERICAN TECHNIQUE

RATES: One day class $6.50—Two day class $11.50—Six day class $28.50—One hour private lesson $10.00 by appointment.

JOIN YOUR CLASS DAILY AT THE SKI SCHOOL BELL—9:30

SKI SCHOOL

Newcomers drifted into town on bikes, buses, or in old sedans with skis sticking out the windows. They looked around, decided to spend the night, and never left. Some had money to burn while others mopped floors to buy dinner. A reporter described Vail as "a human mix of part cowboy, part ski-bum, part Grosse Pointe and Boston blue blood."

Rich, poor, or somewhere in between, Vail's first residents shared one common trait: they were all from somewhere else. No one could brag that his grandfather had owned the grocery store or the bank. Strangers in a new land, they formed strong attachments to one another and to the little village not yet on the Colorado map. But in the first year a question hung over the town. Would Vail get off the ground?

No one questioned the success of the mountain. Skiers loved it. Even a complaint made by a nationally-known skier that Vail did not have enough terrain for experts turned to Vail's advantage. "Our phones rang off the hook," said Parker, "Beginning and intermediate skiers called, people who'd been intimidated by tough runs at Alta and Sun Valley and Aspen, and when they found out that Vail wasn't all steep terrain, they made reservations on the spot."

When the United States Olympic Team arrived for a training camp a week after Vail opened, Parker made sure that the press arrived with them, although the weather conditions were nothing to write about. The racers formed chain gangs to haul snow out of the woods in bushel baskets and pack it on the race course. When the snow finally fell, the temperature fell with it and the Olympians raced their daily 30 miles of downhill in numbing cold. They used up any leftover energy on New Year's Eve, when the town threw a party in their honor with candle-lit gondola cars and a dance band at Mid-Vail.

Only three major lifts served skiers that first winter: the gondola out of the village, a chairlift out of Mid-Vail, and another out of the Back Bowls. Swingsville, Zot, and Ramshorn brought skiers from the mountaintop back to Mid-Vail while combinations of Riva Ridge, Tourist Trap, Pickeroon, Lodgepole Gulch, International, and Bear Tree took them to the village. Early Vail skiers recalled that three days after a snowstorm they could still find plenty of untracked powder on the mountain.

Joe Staufer, aided by several young people drawn to Vail strictly for the skiing, ran the restaurant at Mid-Vail. They started the day with Joe but often disappeared by lunchtime. "You have to do a *little* work," he complained. "But we came here to *ski*," they insisted.

Vail attracted so few paying customers on weekdays that the eight instructors in the ski school often skied alone. Ticket sellers carried the days' receipts to the Vail Associates' offices in a brown paper shopping bag. On some days, had the money been stolen, it wouldn't have made much difference.

U.S. Ski Team at Alpine Training Camp in December, 1964, top, and Bob Parker in the gates. (Vail Associates and Barry Stott Photos)

One morning Peter Seibert carefully counted all the people on the mountain and found 38 paying guests and 50 employees, a total of 88 people skiing Vail's seven square miles of terrain. Vail's on-mountain capacity of 1,500 skiers had been reached only six times by the spring of 1964. But one day in March, 231 skiers overwhelmed the ski school, and on another day later in the month, 1,976 people were on the mountain. The gondola line stretched in long curls outside the terminal and

The Return of the Utes

As Vail's second ski season approached, the fall weather resembled the first season — a depressing cycle of blue-sky days that had managers frowning. One day in November, Peter Seibert, Bob Parker, and Dick Hauserman discussed the matter. Parker recalled fragments of their rambling conversation.

"We oughta have somebody do a rain dance for us . . . Except it would have to be a snow dance . . . Who could do something like that?"

As it turned out, Dick Hauserman had a friend who once worked on the Ute Indian Reservation in southwestern Colorado. He asked her whether the Utes did snow dances. She wasn't sure but suggested calling Eddie Box of the Bear Clan, who handled ceremonial dances.

Bob Parker called Eddie Box and asked him if the Utes did snow dances. They didn't. Did they do rain dances? They did. Well, would they consider doing a rain dance and calling it a snow dance? Box told Parker he'd have to check that out with Minnie Cloud of the Cloud Clan, their senior person with connections to the weather gods.

When Minnie Cloud allowed as how a snow dance might be arranged, Parker let the press in on it. "The scheduled dance is actually a rain dance," he announced. "However, tribe officials have given approval to a temporary change of nomenclature, and the dance will be called a snow dance this one time only.

"Because of the temperatures at Vail, we are very hopeful that the dance will produce snow rather than rain," Parker added. "Rain, of course, would be disastrous, but we're willing to take that chance."

On December 9, a caravan of Southern Utes pulled up to the entrance of The Lodge where Vail officials lined up to greet them. Eddie Box, a man of ramrod stature with a handshake that crushed bone, emerged from his Cadillac followed by the diminutive and dignified Minnie Cloud and a dozen Ute dancers.

The Utes danced on the deck at The Lodge in a bitterly cold wind under gray skies. The next day the sun returned as they rode the gondola up the mountain where a crowd had gathered at Mid-Vail. With the Gore Range as a backdrop, the Utes began to dance, and Minnie Cloud stretched her hands to the sky and chanted fervent prayers to her weather gods. Eddie Box urged the audience to join them, and soon both Indians and skiers danced in swaying circles under a clear blue sky.

The Utes departed, leaving behind high hopes for the swift arrival of powder snow. That was on December 11.

The sky arched smooth and blue for the next two days. Bob Parker called Eddie Box on December 14 and mentioned, in a friendly way, that it had not snowed. "Don't worry," said Eddie, "Minnie says she can feel it coming."

It clouded over on December 15 and the clouds thickened the next day. Finally, on December 17, a blizzard launched the ski season. ■

kept skiers waiting 20 minutes.

No sooner had Vail celebrated those record-breaking days when it faced its first serious crisis.

The first day of April, 1964, dawned clear, but by mid-afternoon lowering clouds came swiftly over the mountain. Fourteen-year-old Martin Koether, visiting from Illinois with his aunt, skied alone down the Minturn Mile from the top of Chair 4. At a point along the ridge, he should have dropped back down into Mid-Vail. Confused in the dim light of the approaching storm, he turned the other way instead and skied into Game Creek Bowl, which was at that time outside the ski area boundary. By the time the chairlifts closed, Martin had wandered far beyond the sweep of the ski patrol.

When Martin's aunt reported him missing late that afternoon, the Vail Ski Patrol called in searchers and quickly organized a rescue plan. As the gondola rumbled back into action, the spring storm struck the darkening mountain with blizzard force.

By that time, Martin Koether found himself near the bottom of Game Creek in deep snow and deep trouble. He abandoned his skis, struggled through the waist-deep snow for a short distance, and realized he had no chance to make it back to the ridgetop that night. Wisely, he burrowed into the snow under the bushy shelter of spruce tree branches. There, cold, wet, and frightened, he eventually fell asleep.

Meanwhile, teams of rescuers methodically searched the face of Vail Mountain. When they found nothing, they went beyond the boundaries. A few of them actually dropped into Game Creek, calling and listening. But they heard only the storm.

At 3 a.m., exhausted, grim-faced rescuers returned from the search. Martin's father had been called and was on his way from Chicago. Word of the lost boy went out and volunteers converged on Vail, spreading out again to search the mountain in the day's first light. By that time, their hope for Martin's survival had dimmed.

Martin not only survived the storm but slept so soundly he didn't hear the shouts of the rescue team in Game Creek. At daylight, he left his snowcave and began a wearying six-hour climb to the ridgetop. Later that day, amazed rescuers found him, very cold and tired, walking his way to safety.

Although Martin Koether's snowcave survival was the most dramatic, it was not the only such story in Vail. In December, 1964, a seven-year-old Dodge sedan with Ohio license plates rattled into town and pulled up next to a high snowbank on one side of a public parking lot. Art and Jim unrolled their sleeping bags and curled up for the night in the Dodge.

They wandered around Vail the next day, found it to their liking, and took jobs — Jim as a bartender, Art on the lift crew. With payday at least a week off, they spent another night in their cramped but inexpensive parking lot lodge. By the third night, snowplows had piled so much snow up against the car they had to shovel their way into it. Still, they found the price of car-lodging hard to beat and stayed on. Then one night the temperature plunged to 40 below zero, and Art and Jim nearly froze to death.

The time had come to find better quarters, but they hated the thought of spending more money. So they pushed open the door on the

The Red Lion Inn, top, as it looked in 1963 (Ted Bischoff Photo). His family rejoices as "lost boy" Martin Koether returns after his overnight ordeal in Game Creek Bowl.

The Brown family: Cindy, Todd, Mike, Vi, and Byron, early 1970s.

far side of the Dodge, dug a small room in the wall of snow beyond, and set up private residence in the public parking lot for the rest of the winter.

Each night, they crawled through the car into their snowbank bedroom. They rose early to wash in hotel rest rooms and persuaded some of the girls at The Lodge to do their laundry for them. They worked on through the winter, well rested and in excellent health. Their only serious setback occurred when a plow packed snow so solidly around the car one night that they couldn't get the door open. But they managed to get the window open and dug their way out by hand.

When the spring thaw melted their snowcave, Art moved on, but Jim stayed to start his own business and to look for better housing. Soon after he moved into a heated room with comfortable bed and hot shower, he caught a cold.

Dick Dixon started life in the resort with a bang. "I got into Vail in January of 1963," he said. "I walked up to the Red Lion to get a beer and apply for a job. I put my hand on the door handle and the door blew open, knocking me flat on the ground. They'd had a natural gas explosion inside."

Dixon worked as a waiter for the Red Lion, a job that brought him not only a paycheck but a ski pass, a place to live, and all his meals. Later he joined Vail's police force, which consisted of a few citizens appointed by the county as deputy sheriffs and paid by Vail Associates.

In those days, policemen spent most of their time tracking down stolen skis and keeping obstreperous drinkers in line. A few locals gave them a hard time whenever they got a chance. "In a town where everyone knew everyone else," said Dixon, "some people would push you as far as they could. I remember one time over at The Casino it took four guys to help me get handcuffs on one of 'em, and then I had to drag him down the stairs backwards. One of our cops, though, didn't taken anything from anybody — he was a cowboy from Derby Mesa and he had a grip like a trap — so when we had a problem with locals we tried to send him.

"But there was one Sunday," explained Dixon, "when I got this hysterical phone call — somebody yelling that there was a gun fight on the main street of Vail. So I put on my gun and I went down the street and I could hear this firing was very, very steady. Six shots and then they quit. Then six more.

"There were some infamous characters living upstairs from where Gorsuch is now. Across the street, which was dirt at that time, there was a Coke bottle leaning up against the wall of the liquor store. And these guys were shooting at that Coke bottle, right in downtown Vail at 11 o'clock on Sunday morning. So I walked upstairs and we had a little chat. And we didn't have any more shooting on the streets of Vail."

Since it had no golf course, tennis courts, or swimming pools to attract summer visitors, Vail advertised steak fries, pack trips, and the fact that a three-pound German Brown had been hooked out of Gore Creek. Local residents relished the warm weather. "Winter is why we came here," they said, "but summer is why we stayed."

Vail Associates planned to close The Lodge the first summer, but Joe Staufer, promising to round up guests and run the place on a low budget, convinced them not to.

"I had this ridiculously cheap weekend package," said Joe. "For $10.00, you got a gondola ride, dinner and lodging, and breakfast the next morning. Mid-Vail didn't have a liquor license so everyone brought his own booze, and the local people helped out by busing tables and cleaning up.

"I had no night auditor," he went on, "so I slept next to the switchboard at night, and I cooked breakfast for the guests in the morning. During the week we couldn't afford to fire up the boiler for the kitchen because it took too much gas, so I put charcoal in the fireplace and cooked steaks and lamb chops and trout for the dinner guests. It was a shoestring operation and very hard work, but people loved it, and they still remember those days because they had so much fun."

People moved to Vail on a whim or on the spur of the moment. Vi and Byron Brown, die-hard skiers from Denver, longed to live in the mountains. One day in the summer of 1964, Byron noticed a sign reading LOTS FOR SALE IN VAIL in the window of a Littleton real estate office. He went in and spoke to the agent, "If you can find me a place to live up there, I'll sell those lots for you."

The Browns moved to a house in West Vail that August with their two boys and a third child on the way. The gas hadn't been hooked up, the windows weren't in, and the only running water was in the creek. Field mice overran the house in such numbers that Vi kept all their food, not just the perishables, in the refrigerator. But Vi and Byron felt they'd moved to heaven.

Another family sent word to friends in the East. "So here we are in Vail, Colorado," they wrote. "The place looks like a movie set for Heidi, and we feel like strangers in paradise. We have no phone, no radio reception, no television, no trash pick-up, no newspaper delivery. The electricity keeps going off. The house is wonderful, but odd — built into the side of a hill. The bedroom is enormous, but the dining room

*E*arly Vail golfers, top. So early, in fact, that one might question whether a golf course yet existed. Above, a weekend deal at The Lodge at Vail in 1963. (Vail Associates Photos)

The Joys of Skiing

PHOTOS BY BARRY STOTT

Making Mountains

KEN REDDING

Rocky Mountain geology — with its millions of years of ocean flooding, worn ancestral ranges, and all the folds, fractures, thrusts, and wrinkles that indicate earth's endless rearrangements — defies simplification. But from the top of Vail Mountain, the skier comes into contact, at least, with a few illustrations.

The magnificent peaks seen from there — the Gore Range and the Sawatch Range — are faulted anticlines, or fractured upthrusts of granite, scoured and sculptured by glacial ice into canyons and pinnacles that dazzle the eye and thrill the soul but are far too rugged for skiing.

Whereas Vail Mountain, the humble cousin ridge between the two ranges, is perfect for skiing, formed as it was, not from upthrusts, but from deposits. Layers of mud and sand washed down from prehistoric mountains into prehistoric seas and accumulated to depths of thousands of feet. The sandstone cliffs of the South Rim Runs and under Chair 4 are part of this buildup; so are the limestone outcrops like the wall at the head of China Bowl.

The soft rocks of Vail Mountain were molded by rainfall and runoff. Over the centuries, these erosive forces created the valley of Two Elk Creek and the Back Bowls, along with Mill Creek and the Mid-Vail Bowl.

The north side of the mountain has been dramatically affected by landslides. There are several places where Chairs 2, 9, and 17 pass over hummocky debris that slid away from firmer rocks, creating the interesting dropoffs and runouts of such runs as the Ledges, Minnie's Mile, Avanti, and Pickeroon.

The scar of a slide in the early 1980s can be seen by the observant skier above the road that leads from Riva Ridge to the Internationals, proving that even mountains shaped by millions of years can suddenly rearrange themselves, and that geological forces on Vail Mountain are still at work. ■

is smaller than our dining room table. The living room windows go all the way to the ceiling and the view is terrific, but downstairs in the back of the house are three bedrooms that have no windows at all — we could grow mushrooms there.

"We hear there is a dentist in Glenwood Springs, 65 miles west through a canyon, a veterinarian in Leadville, 40 miles south over Battle Mountain, and everything else is in Denver, 100 miles east over Loveland Pass, which is almost 12,000 feet high. This place takes getting used to. But it certainly is beautiful."

From the beginning, two Vails existed — one a posh and polished ski resort with celebrities and cocktail parties, and the other a community of people who did without phones and running water. Two Vails, separated, but inseparable. One built the other.

Vail's most enduring architectural symbols — the Clock Tower and the Covered Bridge — were built in 1965. The architectural review board, thinking the Clock Tower would probably be the highest structure ever built in town, approved it only after intense deliberation.

Two Vermonters, John and Cissy Dobson, built their Covered Bridge Store next to a bridge over Gore Creek that Vail Associates intended to cover. "Then fall came," said Cissy, "and we were ready to open and the bridge wasn't covered. I'm not sure it ever would have been, so we got together with Vail Associates and split the cost of putting a roof on it so our store name would have some meaning."

The Dobsons produced a Colorado version of a Vermont general store. "At that time, Vail was mostly ski shops and gifts shops," said Cissy, "but at our store you could buy all kinds of housewares and hardware and ordinary clothes like the old shrink-to-fit Levis that cost $5.98. We even carried underwear. There was excitement when the word got out that we were going to carry bras — women hadn't been able to buy a bra in town for all that time."

Vail's first baby was born to Vail mountain founder Earl Eaton and his wife, Penny, in 1965. They planned that the delivery would take place in Leadville, but on January 21 those plans changed quickly.

The chairlift out of Mid-Vail broke down that day, stalling skier traffic terribly and demanding immediate attention. It meant an all-night repair job for Earl Eaton. He took a break at midnight and used a ski patrol phone to call his wife. Everything was fine, of course, since the baby wasn't due for another two weeks. But right after Earl's call Penny's labor started and soon she knew that a trip to Leadville was out of the question. A few hours later, a doctor on temporary duty in Vail delivered a baby boy at a tiny clinic in the Mill Creek building while father Earl worked until dawn when the ski patrol brought him the good news.

By 1966, Peter Seibert realized he was managing both a ski resort

VAIL TRAIL PHOTO

*S*ummers in early Vail were quiet except for an occasional rodeo. (Photos by Vail Trail, left, Barry Stott, right, and Vail Associates, bottom)

and a town, and the combination took too much time. "We were trying to form the structure of a community," he said, "but some people liked things the way they were. They liked the benevolent dictatorship — one man running things for them. It was easy; there was no law. But dogs were running loose so I started locking them up and charging the owners room and board. In a little community where there were no rules or regulations, I ended up having to be dog catcher."

Seibert had enough on his hands without having to worry about stray dogs. In spite of the resort's popularity, Vail Associates struggled to keep its financial head above water. "The problems we had raising money to get Vail started were nothing compared to the ones we had those first years after it started," said George Caulkins. Vail suffered the same problems that hounded other ski resorts: winter and spring with crowds of skiers and full cash registers followed by summer and fall with vacant streets and empty pockets.

"We were all signing notes guaranteeing Vail's credit," said Caulkins, "and Vail really didn't have any credit."

Meanwhile, the village needed roads paved, water piped, schools built, doctors hired, sewers drained, and dogs tied up. Vail Associates could no longer foot the bill for those services. Clearly, the time had come to separate the ski operation from the town.

Incorporation, however, brought its own problems. "We had to cheat a little bit," said Rod Slifer. "The Colorado statutes said you had to have 100 people living within a square mile in order to incorporate. We didn't have that many. But we talked 20 people into going together to buy two lots at the other end of town, and that way we ended up with 50 people living within a half square mile."

In 1966, a community of skiers became the Town of Vail. A mayor and town council met each Monday evening to ponder municipal issues, and when television reception came to the valley, the council moved its meetings to Tuesday.

After all those years without Monday night football, who wanted to miss it?

GROWING

UP

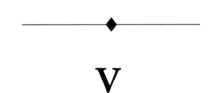

V

AYOR JOHN DOBSON, straight-faced and diligent, tended his municipal duties and properly greeted dignitaries from all over the world. Then he went home, took up his pen, and poked fun at all of it, himself included.

Dobson began writing melodramas in 1966 under the penname Gregory Beresford Skeffington and gave them such titles as "Dirty Doings at the Depot" and "Aunty Bellum's Last Stand." He wrote them in one act, fearing his audience would not return if he gave them an intermission, and he and his Vail Players staged them each summer at The Lodge.

Vail supplied Dobson with all the material he could use. The rich and the famous, in-laws, outlaws, and town squabbles — all were grist for the Dobson mill. Actors and audiences, first fortifying themselves at the bar, participated in these cultural evenings with high enthusiasm.

As Vail grew from tiny town to international resort, Dobson played the best of all possible roles: he provided leadership and comic relief. Vail needed plenty of both. Its rise to stardom was as melodramatic as one of Dobson's productions. Vail welcomed its millionth skier at the ticket office in the spring of 1968.

The next year Vail Associates borrowed the name Lionshead from a rock outcropping above the nearby town of Minturn and opened up Game Creek Bowl on the back side of the mountain and Simba, Bwana, and Born Free on the front side. The Lionshead base area featured the clustered concrete look of French resorts like Chamonix and Les Arcs.

When Lionshead was dedicated, an African lion named Simba took part in the ceremonies. Simba, tethered by chain to his anxious trainer, stalked quietly over the snow and up the steps of the lower gondola terminal. At the doorway, he brushed a loose wire in a string of Christmas lights. Slightly shocked, Simba leaped into the building and made several lunges toward the crowd before his trainer settled him.

Peter Seibert declined an offer to ride up the mountain with the lion but agreed to sit with him in a gondola car for photographers. Simba entered the car, gazed at Seibert, and belched deeply. Seibert got out. The attendant locked the car door and Simba, with jungle dignity, rode out of the terminal accompanied by his trainer.

With the addition of Lionshead, Vail advertised a resort with seven chairlifts, two gondolas, four beginners' lifts, 28 restaurants, 4,500 beds, a ski school with 70 instructors, and an all-day lift ticket costing $8. Said Seibert, "In a few years, Vail will be a bustling town 10 months out of the year. And when that happens, we will need the other two months to recuperate — in someone else's resort."

Seibert's prediction came true faster than anyone had expected as growth in the valley raced to keep up with growth on the mountain.

In 1963, Colorado had passed a law that allowed the sale of "air

Simba the lion added spark to dedication ceremonies at the Lionshead gondola terminal, shown below under construction in 1969. (Vail Associates Photos)

rights," or condominium spaces, over land held in common. The condominium law fanned the flames of mountain real estate all over Colorado. Skiers could buy a condominium for a quarter of what a house might cost. Reported *The Denver Post* in July, 1964: "A whole new group of persons, not necessarily rich or looking for a tax write-off, find that they can own a condominium in the Rockies as a second home, use it as they wish and make money from it when they're away. It's a new concept in Colorado tourism and the cash registers are ringing."

Most people who bought real estate in Vail simply wanted a home in a ski area, but Vail's quick success brought buyers who wanted mountain property as an investment. With limited land in the Gore Creek Valley, prices soared as "a condo in Vail" became something of a status symbol.

"That was in the mid-1960s," said Rod Slifer. "One day this fellow came in from New York and looked at a unit in Manor Vail and said he'd like to buy it. He asked me how much. I told him $75,000. I started writing up the contract, but before I got it done he handed me a check for the whole amount. It was incredible in those years — there was no negotiation on price. That was it. Bang. If that guy didn't take it, the next guy would."

As success exploded all around them, Vail residents faced the dual challenge of running a booming resort as well as fostering such community institutions as school, church, bank, and medical facility. In Vail's early years, those institutions took shelter wherever they could find it and moved from place to place like street peddlers as the town grew. The Vail Mountain School held classes in 11 different locations before settling permanently on the site of the old Baldauf homestead east of town. The church, bank, and public school moved almost as often. So did the medical facilities.

In 1965, Dr. Tom Steinberg began his long association with Vail residents, and since the nearest veterinarian lived 40 miles away, he also cared for their pets. One day the game warden brought him a golden eagle with a bullet wound in its chest. Tom kept one of his human patients waiting while he treated the eagle, and when the man complained, Tom put it to him squarely: "There are a lot more of your kind around here than there are golden eagles. The eagle comes first."

Before the building of the Interfaith Chapel, Catholics celebrated Mass at The Casino in the stale air left over from Saturday night ski patrol parties. Protestants worshipped among bent straws and dirty glasses in the Golden Ski Room at The Lodge. When religious groups began fund-raising for the chapel, a bartender at Donovan's Copper Bar put jars of his own homemade pickled eggs out on the bar, labeled them "Pickled Eggs for God," and raised enough money to donate a pew. When The Bank of Vail was built next to the chapel, a local wag asked

New York Mayor Lindsay, participant at Vail's first Symposium, chats with Vail Mayor John Dobson. The Vail Ski School and Ski Patrol, shown here in 1971, facing page, grew right along with Vail.

which building would get the "Jesus Saves" sign.

In the summer of 1971, the town invited state and national community leaders to its first symposium. The audience traveled by gondola to the sessions at Eagle's Nest, where New York City Mayor John Lindsay quipped that he felt ill at ease at that elevation, breathing air that he couldn't see.

For the two days of the symposium, Vail examined its role as a mountain resort in an urbanized America.

"Your community is much larger than just the people who are here now," said Robert Knecht, mayor of Boulder, Colorado. "Many of us feel an interest and a stake in it. I come here as a skier, but I also come here as a person concerned with cities and as a Coloradan who wants to see the very best happen here."

The very best did not always happen. As the boom continued, speculators cashed in on Vail, and residents discovered that success was something to cope with rather than crow about. Said Joe Staufer, "The people who came here first were committed to building Vail; we all worked together to create that dream. But there was a wave of people who came after Vail was successful, and they came for the buck. And that's the only motivation they had."

During the 1970s, backhoes and bulldozers eviscerated meadow and hillside and piled up dark, wet earth where condominiums emerged like mushrooms from some ancient mycelium. Some residents retreated to the relative peace and quiet of the city. Said one man after visiting a Denver suburb: "It sure was quiet there. I couldn't help thinking how nice it was to be in a place that was finished."

On winter weekends, thousands of skiers drove down the interstate ramps looking for a place to park, a short lift line, or a seat in a restau-

*D*obson cartoon comments on Vail's narrowing view corridors; skiers comment on seasonal preferences. (Photo by Don Simonton)

rant. Sadly, the air that Mayor Lindsay enjoyed could sometimes be seen as smog hanging over the valley on cold winter days.

Those who worked in Vail searched long and hard for affordable housing. Some camped out in vans or tents, shared cramped apartments, or even rented floor space for their sleeping bags. To make ends meet, they held two or three jobs during the ski season and barely survived the months between winter and summer jobs.

"We didn't realize how long it was between the end of the ski season and the beginning of the construction job in the summer," said ski instructor Bob Dorf. "Our money ran out in May, and we had to borrow from home. One year we were saved when my wife, Patty, found one of my old paychecks in her cookbook. She was using it to mark hamburger recipes."

The disillusioned took their damaged dreams and moved on to easier living in the greener fields of Montana or Alaska. But others had fallen in love with the valley, the mountain, and the people. Whatever its problems, Vail was home.

By the spring of 1976, Vail's 14-year mountain operation had given five million skiers some 14 million lift rides without any major mishap. But on the morning of March 26, a tragic gondola accident killed four people and injured eight more.

The day dawned bright and warm as crowds of skiers lined up at the lifts. At Lionshead, red and yellow gondola cars swung steadily out of the lower terminal.

Near Tower 5, two-thirds of the way up the mountain and out of sight of both upper and lower terminals, the top gondola cable had frayed. The unraveled wires jammed the wheeled carriage assembly of one gondola car and partially derailed it. But the lower cable kept mov-

Snow Stats

CLIFF SIMONTON

S tatistics, they say, don't prove a thing. Nevertheless, they're fun to ponder, revealing, as they do, amusing or downright quirky bits of information.

Such is the case with a 13-page computer printout of snowfall analysis for Vail Mountain. These statistics date from 1963 (Vail's second season) through the spring of 1986 — 23 years of ski seasons which usually began at Thanksgiving and ended around April 15, although those dates varied.

Over 23 ski seasons, 7,095 inches of snow fell on Vail Mountain, an average of 308.5 inches per year, not counting the storms that provided the pre-season base. But the snowfall varied. During five of those years, it added up to over 400 inches, the 1977-1978 season an all-time winner with 473 inches. Then came the lean seasons — three of them scattered over the years — with less than 200 inches.

Worst marks go to 1980-1981, when only 171 inches fell, a barren winter with unnerving stretches of blue sky. From December 25 to January 25 only three inches of snow drifted down on the mountain.

Two years later, in 1983, the trend reversed and there seemed no way to turn the stuff off. With the exception of December 1, it snowed every day from November 18 through December 28 — 40 days of pure heaven for powder buffs.

Consistent snowfall rather than huge storms seems to characterize Vail Mountain. On only six days out of 23 seasons did a single snowfall measure over 20 inches. April 10, 1974 took first prize with a 24-inch drop.

The hero date, however, is March 3, when it has snowed for 17 out of the 23 seasons. It has also snowed for 17 years on December 24, 30, and 31, but March 3 has brought the most snowfall — a total of 98 inches.

On the other hand, if you're planning a picnic, consider April 15. In all of Vail's seasons, it has only snowed once on that date — a mere two inches back in 1970.

So much for statistics, which prove only one thing when it comes to snowfall on Vail Mountain. Deep or light, dump or trace, the stuff keeps coming down. ■

ing and literally sawed through the holding arm. The car fell 100 feet into the snow, leaving its severed carriage assembly on the cable. The next car hit the assembly, derailed, and also fell. A third car, partially derailed, slid back into the car behind it.

By that time, the gondola had stopped. The last derailed car, its six occupants shocked motionless, hung by a strip of metal from the cable. And 215 other people were stranded in 39 gondola cars.

As the first rescuers rushed to the scene, ski patrolman Chupa Nelson heard the report on his radio and thought "Who's kidding who?" When he heard another report seconds later, he headed for Lionshead.

"We knew right away we'd have to evacuate the gondola," said Nelson. "We'd practiced the procedure for years and years, but we never thought it would happen."

Every Vail ski patrolman learned to ride "the bike," an aluminum-frame gadget designed to hook over the gondola cable and glide from car to car. Although the cable was 210 feet off the ground in some places, many patrolmen found the procedure entertaining. "We got so good at riding those bikes that we used to have drag races on the cables," said Nelson. "We made a game out of it."

But on that Friday in March the game turned deadly serious. Nelson, with the 40-pound bike strapped over one shoulder and 30 pounds of goldline climbing rope over the other, climbed the 120-foot tower above the derailed car. "About halfway up," he said, "I could see that the entire car was hanging by a thread of metal half an inch long and no thicker than a pencil.

"I got the bike on the cable, looped the rope around my waist, and started down the cable very, very slowly, just inching along because I was afraid of what even a little vibration might do to that car. I stopped the bike a few inches from the car and reassured the people that everything was going to be fine, which I wasn't at all sure of because if a wind had come up or if someone had moved the wrong way that car would have gone down."

With infinite care Nelson secured the car to the cable and the tower with both rope and chain. "Then I climbed through the window," he said. "It was pretty cramped with seven of us in there, but I sat down and introduced myself and said, 'We're home free.' Some of them were weeping."

With the derailed car secure, 25 patrolmen began evacuating the other cars. They worked in teams of three, one man riding the bike from car to car and lowering skiers by rope in basket-like seats while two patrolmen guided the ropes from below. Meanwhile, other mountain crews and townspeople mobilized to provide medical aid, transportation, communication, and food.

The patrolmen worked themselves into a state of numb exhaustion

*P*atrolman Chupa Nelson, facing page, secures damaged gondola car to cable with chain and rope. Above, slippery footing, small work space, and dizzying heights make getting on the rescue "bike" no easy task. This early photo taken on Vail's original gondola. (Photos by Peter Runyon)

TRAIL CONSTRUCTION

*T*rees are cut, sorted, and trucked to the nearest mill. Remaining wood is burned before bulldozers move in to remove tree stumps and grade the run to its final shape. The disturbed soil is then seeded, fertilized and covered with straw mulch to prevent erosion. (Vail Associates Photos)

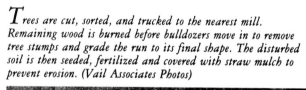

CHAIRLIFT INSTALLATION

The pouring of foundation cement and placement of heavy lift tower components are accomplished with helicopters especially equipped for operation at high altitudes. The adjustment of sheave wheels and attachment of individual chairs completes the project. (Vail Associates Photos)

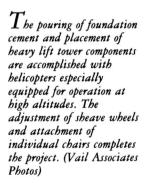

but retrieved all 215 people without injury in the seven-hour rescue. The only interference came from three low-flying Denver television news helicopters whose noisy rotors fouled up communications and created dangerous downdrafts on the cable.

The next summer Vail Associates installed a new gondola system with sophisticated safety features that made it virtually impossible for any such accident to happen again.

During the 1970s and 1980s, Vail settled down to pave its streets, cover its parking lots, flower its borders, and polish its image as international resort. Its institutions found homes in their own buildings. A Safeway store and small shopping mall sprouted up a few miles west of town. Vail annexed both ends of the valley, creating a long, skinny island of a town completely surrounded by Forest Service land.

As a municipality, Vail resembled other towns. It provided police and fire protection, parks and recreation, sewer and water, and generally tended to the health, safety, and welfare of its approximately 5,000 citizens. As a resort, however, it faced the onslaught of crowds that quadrupled its population several times a year. Those visitors provided the town with an enviable tax base but required giant expenditures in return. By 1984, the town budget totaled $11.5 million.

"Most other cities with that kind of budget would have a population of 25,000," said Rich Caplan, then town manager. "But we have far more issues to worry about than most towns of 5,000 because that number can go to 22,000 or more, and we have to be prepared.

"As a town manger, I feel like a farmer sometimes," he continued. "We're as dependent on good snow to keep our business running as the farmer is on good weather to make his crops grow. If we have a good snow, we'll have a good season. Bad snow, a bad season."

Yet, as John Dobson once said, "Vail has problems other towns would pay to have."

In 1982, the resort celebrated its 20th anniversary and for one week in January rolled back the cost of a lift ticket to the original 1962 price of $5. On the day the special price began, cars jammed the I-70 off-ramp and backed up traffic for two miles.

In 20 years, Vail had grown far beyond the hopes and dreams and deprivations of its pioneers. Vail Valley residents could now purchase everything from a garden hose to a washing machine, disposable diapers to radial tires. The clinic had long since posted a discreet sign, "We No Longer Treat Pets."

The old saying that in May you could fire a cannon up Bridge Street without worrying about hitting anyone no longer applied. Peter Seibert's vision of a bustling resort had come true, even the part about recuperating in someone else's resort. Worn-out residents regularly rested in Mexico and Hawaii.

The real estate market softened and settled but still produced a story or two. One of the Mill Creek Circle lots in the original 1962 filing first sold for approximately $5,000, and a house went up on it. In 1983, an investor bought the property for $1.2 million and tore down the house. In 1985, the empty lot came back on the market for $2.5 million.

As for investments, those who danced to George Caulkins' tune back in 1961 had reason to love him. By 1986, their $10,000 investment in

It's Never Too Late

Everyone pictures the classic "never-ever" as the three or four-year-old child sliding wobbly-kneed down a patch of snow into his parent's waiting arms.

But consider never-ever Pressley Walker of Jacksonville, Florida, who contemplated the skiing scene and said: "If you understand the principle, it looks like it would be pretty easy." In December, 1984, he took his first lesson. He was 76 years old.

Walker might have retired from the sport that very day, having taken top honors as Vail's eldest never-ever, but as it turned out, he understood the principle, found it easy, and has returned twice each year for ski vacations. "He promises to quit at noon, but he never does," said his daughter, Beth Slifer.

Walker proved not only his own point but another one: that it's never too late to start, even when it comes to skiing. ■

the non-existent ski area had reached a value of more than $500,000.

Not everyone enjoyed Vail's slick new image. Some felt saddened at the sight of homey, brown and white Tyrolean buildings standing in the shadow of eight-story concrete condominiums. They questioned why the yearly symposium moved off the mountain into windowless conference rooms and no longer addressed subjects unique to resorts. They were angry that Vail seemed to have traded the last of its Western look for the sleek, bland look of a country club.

But the gains were greater than the losses. "I see Vail as a place to live," said Rod Slifer. "We've created a community with schools and a hospital and kids graduating from high school and going away and some of them coming back now to become a part of the community." And from Vail founder Jack Tweedy: "I have a lot of old friends who decry the density and the height of the buildings and the fact that they can't find any friends in the lift lines. But that's the penalty you pay for success."

Vail counted with pride the symbols of its growth. It opened in 1962 with 300 beds for guests. In 1982, it offered 20,000. The occupants of those 20,000 beds could chose to dine in any of 104 restaurants in an area that extended west to the town of Edwards. They could ride 25 lifts to ski terrain on two mountains, tee off on five 18-hole golf courses, swim in countless aquamarine pools, check out books from a $2.4 million earth-sheltered library, and skate at an Olympic-sized ice arena.

The ice arena had been named for John Dobson, who endured and enjoyed Vail's growth during his nine years as mayor.

He had welcomed a group of Chinese writers, squired them around town, and listened to lengthy and eloquent pre-banquet toasts, all in Chinese. He delighted a flock of Russian city planners by sharing his golf clubs with them; they used the clubs like hockey sticks, then rushed out onto the driving range to retrieve the balls they hit.

"IF THAT CATCHES ON WE COULD ALL BE IN FOR A HEAP O' TROUBLE"

He soothed the ruffled feathers of Mill Creek Circle residents when Elvis Presley and friends rented a house there and spent the nights roaring around the neighborhood on snowmobiles. When a Denver Cadillac dealer later called to say that Elvis Presley had purchased a car for the mayor, Dobson declined the offer and suggested to Presley that he donate the car to charity.

The same Mill Creek Circle folks smiled proudly when Gerald R. Ford and his family resided in their midst but mourned the loss of their privacy and rankled under the strict attention of the Secret Service. Dobson described their plight in a melodrama number titled "The Mill Creek Circle Blues."

Although Dobson retired as mayor in 1976, he stayed involved in the community and enjoyed one of Vail's finest, real-life melodramas: the Oldenburg sculpture controversy.

In 1981, the Vail Town Council commissioned pop artist Claes Oldenburg to create a major sculpture for Vail. Oldenburg came west, wandered around town getting a feel for the place, and returned to New York. Later, for the sum of $10,000, Vail received a model of the proposed work. Over a section of Lionshead, Oldenburg planned to arch a 60-foot high orange fishing pole, its line descending into Gore Creek, there attached to an object the size of a 50-gallon drum with jagged lid representing a rusted tin can.

Vail's *avant-garde* mused over what a Claes Oldenburg sculpture could do for the town's image while environmentalists cringed at the thought of the quintessential symbol for trash in pristine Gore Creek. Oldenburg's price tag of $190,000 caused acid indigestion in some quarters. A rickety caricature of the sculpture appeared downstream at Dowd Junction.

Oldenburg returned to Vail to attend an open town meeting where he explained the illusive beauty of rusted tin. Many spoke fervently on both sides of the issue. The battle raged on until Oldenburg himself brought peace by withdrawing his offer and stating that the climate for one of his sculptures did not exist in Vail at that time. No one argued the point. Oldenburg retrieved his model but kept the $10,000. At Dowd Junction, the caricature remained for years.

John Dobson had a simple solution to the controversy all along. Since the town council also faced the issue of whether or not to use traffic lights in town, he suggested that they simply festoon the Oldenburg fishing pole with red, yellow, and green lights, install it at the four-way stop, and solve two political problems at once.

In November, 1984, at age 67, John Dobson died suddenly of a heart attack. The following year the Vail Institute sponsored "John Dobson Night." Part of the show featured the Vail Players doing bits from the old melodramas. Then, as a spotlight illuminated his empty

*V*ail Village and Vail Mountain, 1984.
(Photo by David Lokey)

director's chair, Dobson's tape-recorded monologues were played. A year after his death, he still had 'em rolling in the aisles.

John Dobson made fun of Vail only as one who knew and loved the place. He often delivered his most telling commentaries about the town through the fictitious Gregory Beresford Skeffington. Shortly before he died, he conducted a tongue-in-cheek interview with Skeffington and ended the piece with an author's note:

"Of course there really is not such a person as Gregory Beresford Skeffington. I made him up — and all the very bad plays he wrote. But the people in them are real, or as real as actors and actresses want to be, and I love them all. Those were great times and a part of growing up with Vail. This growing up process continues, but it's much more serious now.

"The players probably haven't done much for culture, but hopefully, they have reminded us to laugh at ourselves once in a while. This is important for people who don't have much to laugh or smile about, and even more important, perhaps, for those of us in Vail, who do."

BEAVER

CREEK

VI

V

VAIL'S STRUGGLE FOR a Forest Service permit in 1959 seemed only a skirmish compared to the battle that raged over the opening of Beaver Creek.

The controversy began in May, 1970, in Amsterdam, Holland, when the International Olympic Committee (IOC) named Denver as site for the 1976 Winter Olympics. Denverites, thrilled at the opportunity to show off their city, quickly formed the Denver Organizing Committee (DOC) for the huge task of overseeing arrangements for the Games.

The committee's problems began immediately. Sites for various Olympic events had been selected when Denver made its bid to the IOC. Evergreen, a mountain community near Denver, would hold the cross-country skiing, ski jumping, and luge, while alpine events would take place on Mt. Sniktau, an undeveloped mountain just east of the Continental Divide. Or so the DOC thought.

As it turned out, however, many people in Evergreen did not want the Games in their town at all, and others pointed out that Evergreen's unreliable snowfall could not ensure a good base for a cross-country ski track. Snow conditions were no better on the barren, windswept slopes of Mt. Sniktau, but to hold the Games on the Western Slope, where the snow fell reliably and deeply, created a tangle of transportation and communication problems, and even more important to the DOC, it meant that most of the events of the Denver Olympics would not be held in Denver at all. Months went by and opposition mounted, while the DOC, proud host for the 1976 Winter Games, could not even decide where to hold them.

The committee also struggled with the issues of financing and the building of permanent or throw-away facilities. But its biggest problems surfaced when state representatives Richard Lamm and Bob Jackson spoke out in staunch opposition to holding the Games in Colorado at that time.

Lamm called the whole affair environmental insanity. "Everybody talks about handling the Olympics so the environment doesn't suffer," he said, "but we can't even get a land use plan adopted and can't get the billboards taken down. What makes anyone think we can handle anything as big as the Olympics without hurting the country?"

The DOC studied sites near Keystone and Steamboat Springs but found neither satisfactory. Aspen and Copper Mountain offered their slopes. Vail Associates offered to develop the mountain at Beaver Creek, but the DOC feared attacks from environmental groups if they tried to stage events in Beaver Creek's fragile valley. Pressured by a deadline to announce the sites, the DOC sent committeemen to test ski slopes at various resorts. Finally, at the 1972 Winter Games in Sapporo, the DOC announced that the alpine events for the 1976 Olympics would be held at Beaver Creek.

Back in Colorado, the DOC's problems multiplied as fast as its cost-estimates for the Games. Infighting, a lack of clear direction, and bad public relations played right into the hands of its well-organized opponents. By the summer of 1972, Lamm, Jackson, the Sierra Club, and other environmentalists obtained 76,000 names on a petition to put the Olympic question to Colorado voters.

On November 7, 900,000 people turned out for the general elections

THE OLYMPIC BUBBLE

I didn't vote against the Olympic Games. I voted against the politicians and the arrogant organizers. Against their smugness, secrecy and bungling. And against the promoters and hucksters who were jumping in for a fast buck. It's too bad. I think the Olympics themselves could have been really great. I don't expect we'll see another chance like this in a lifetime.   a Colorado voter

A S ELECTION DAYS GO, November 7, 1972, wasn't a bad one in Colorado. Fresh snow covered the ground across most of the state, but the skies and roads were both clear. Close to 900,000 people went to the polls, stood in line, waited and voted.

When the ballots were counted, Referendum Initiative Number 8 had passed by a surprising 3 to 2 margin, a phenomenon both incredible and incomprehensible to observers the world over.

In effect, the voters of Colorado — a state otherwise known as Ski Country USA, the ski capital of America — had summarily rejected the most prestigious winter sports event known to man. The 1976 Winter Olympics had been sent packing. Nothing like this had ever happened — anywhere — since the modern Games were revived in 1896.

The immediate aftermath in Colorado — depending on who one was and where he stood — was one of head shaking, hand shaking, sadness and joy. The usual election night emotions. But as the smoke cleared and the dust settled, a different mood began to emerge. Many of the people who had pushed the Olympics out of Colorado were now a little abashed about the results. They had voted against Denver's Olympic establishment but meant no disrespect for the Games. They had voted against a $2,000,000 boondoggle but meant no offense to the athletes of the world. It was clearly a case of overkill.

It will be months, perhaps years, before many Coloradans even realize what they really did. Nailing the lid on the Olympic coffin will be no easy task, for electoral ghosts have a peculiar way of filtering out of ballot boxes. Day or night.

and voted down the Olympics by a three-to-two margin. Colorado, ski capital of the nation, sent shockwaves throughout the sports world by turning down the chance to welcome the world to its perfectly powdered mountain slopes. Never before in the history of the modern Games had anything like that happened.

The spotlight then fell on Beaver Creek, famous as the valley where the Games would not be held. No one seemed to know much about the place, but the controversy provoked interest in its future as well as its past.

The history of Beaver Creek began in 1882 when George Townsend, a Vermont man, turned 400 acres of valley land into a prosperous ranch. In 1898, Townsend sold the ranch to John and Caroline Howard of Virginia. The Howards built a large house at the entrance to the valley and stayed there until shortly after the turn of the century. Gulling and Olive Offerson then purchased the property, added a wing to the house, and lived there comfortably for years.

In other parts of Beaver Creek, families and a few flighty bachelors farmed patches of hillside land and often lived on the edge of poverty.

Many knew tragedy. One blustery March day in 1938, Annie Holden climbed into her barn loft to gather eggs. Forgetful for a moment, she stepped backwards and fell through the opening in the floor. Men working on a nearby road found her crawling through the snow, severely injured. When she died a few days later, the whole valley mourned.

The Adams family lost their two-year-old boy in Beaver Creek's wild spring runoff. Overwhelmed by grief, the parents hitched up their team one winter morning and drove out of the valley. They left fires burning in two stoves, food in the cupboards, and the table set for breakfast.

Yet even the poorest and loneliest of the pioneers knew the joys of cool green summers, splendid golden autumns, and the companionship

*S*ign at Sapporo in 1972 indicates that the 1976 Olympics will be held in Colorado. Scenes in the Beaver Creek valley during those years give no hint of the controversy that surrounded it. (Photos by Colorado Magazine, top, Don Simonton, above.)

of winter evenings when they took to the moonlit, snowy slopes with sleds, toboggans, and homemade barn wood skis.

Charlie Eaton, logger, farmer, and born tinkerer, rigged a waterwheel beside the creek and used it to power a grindstone, a butter churn, and a hay baler. After puttering with a length of wire and an old motor, he also produced enough current to power electric lights in his cabin. Charlie figured he spent the best years of his life at Beaver Creek.

Beaver Creek farmers, like those on Gore Creek, enjoyed the high profits of lettuce growing in the 1920s, but many called it quits when the market tightened during the Depression.

Gulling Offerson, who owned most of the property in Beaver Creek during those years, died in a car accident in 1941. His son, unable to manage the ranch, sold it in 1950. Willis Nottingham, whose grandparents had settled in Avon in 1887, bought all the land in Beaver Creek and turned the valley into a single, profitable sheep and cattle ranch.

Earl Eaton had his eye on Beaver Creek even before he and Peter Seibert looked at Vail. In 1956, he showed John Burke, district ranger from Minturn, some rough sketches of trails, lifts, sun decks, and shelters. Burke thought the mountain had possibilities, but nothing came of it and a year later Seibert and Eaton decided on Vail. Willis Nottingham continued ranching undisturbed.

But with Vail established, Peter Seibert looked at Beaver Creek with his developer's eye and made a number of friendly visits to Willis's house. "Peter spent a good deal of time with Willis, drinkin' a little whiskey, and howdyin' and chattin' and just reminding him that he was still around," said a friend. "And when Willis felt the urge for more solitude, he got in touch with Peter."

Willis felt that urge when Interstate 70, with its associated condos, second homes, golf courses, dogs, airport, and people, flowed down the Eagle River Valley in his direction. The urge got stronger when ranchers on either side of Beaver Creek sold to developers. In September, 1971, Willis gave Vail Associates an option on his 2,200 acres and found for himself an isolated ranch in northwestern Colorado. In August, 1972, Vail Associates exercised its option and purchased the land. And then, just three months later, Coloradans voted down the Olympics. It seemed, as one reporter put it, that "Vail Associates was up the creek without a permit."

Vail Associates, however, anticipated no permit problems. The Forest Service had studied the mountain terrain all the way from Minturn to McCoy Creek. Their inventory of that area, called the Meadow Mountain Management Unit, listed Beaver Creek as a "good to outstanding" winter sports site.

With the blessing of the Forest Service and without any deadline pressure from the Olympics, Vail Associates planned to develop Beaver Creek in a calm and orderly fashion. "The Forest Service permit should be merely a technical matter," said one of their officials.

The year 1974 started smoothly enough. In January, the Forest Service filed a draft of its environmental impact statement (E.I.S.) for the Meadow Mountain Management Unit. In February, Eagle County approved Vail Associates' development plans for Beaver Creek. In March, Vail Associates applied for a Forest Service permit to develop

3,000 acres of ski terrain, and in April local Forest Service personnel recommended approval of that permit.

But in August, when the Forest Service filed its final environmental impact statement, Beaver Creek development plans blew sky high. Thirteen separate state agencies reviewed the E.I.S. and did not like what they saw. The state claimed that the E.I.S. was inadequate and incomplete and that it failed to resolve the environmental issues at Beaver Creek.

A reporter for a Denver newspaper put it in tougher language: "The state caught the Forest Service and its gypsy band of rambling developers in mid-stride with a devastating review of the final E.I.S." Suddenly, Vail Associates found the pleasant road to the Forest Service permit full of chuckholes.

John Vanderhoof, completing his last month as governor, ordered the Colorado Land Use Commission to review the matter. In two days of public hearings in December, 1974, the Forest Service repeated its claim that Beaver Creek was a good site for recreational development. Vail Associates promised that Beaver Creek would be the most environmentally sensitive resort ever developed in the Rocky Mountains.

But the state got down to specifics. What about toxic ammonia in the Eagle River, sediment in Beaver Creek, calving grounds for the resident elk, auto emissions trapped by air inversions?

Would the history of the valley be recorded and preserved? That was part of the environment, too. And what about the larger questions of growth associated with the development? Could Eagle County, which only recently emerged from a ranching era with its "a-man's-as-good-as-his-word" values, cope with the impact of 40,000 people?

And if it couldn't, were state laws strong enough to stand up under pressure from eager urban developers? Some questions simply couldn't be answered.

The hearings ended with Forest Supervisor Tom Evans asking Regional Forester William Lucas to approve the project and designate

A view of the Offerson ranch in 1929. The hamlet of Avon and the Nottingham ranches are in the valley beyond. By 1950, Willis Nottingham, below, had bought the ranch on Beaver Creek. (Beaver Creek Collection)

Heavy plastic lining keeps stream water clean while it is diverted around a construction site, while a backhoe works on a temporary sediment pond installed to protect natural drainages. In the summer of 1979, work begins on the 300-space underground parking garage . . .

The size of many larger buildings such as The Centennial requires steel girder construction. Tight scheduling keeps builders busy throughout the winter months on buildings like the Village Hall.

BUILDING OF BEAVER CREEK

*. . . which later serves to support the walls of the Village
Hall. By the fall of 1981, the village core is alive with many
building projects.*

*Developments on the mountain keep pace with
village construction. Helicopters deliver bales of
straw to freshly cut ski runs. Straw mulch
shelters the soil during the revegetation process.
The construction of the Spruce Saddle Restaurant
was completed in the fall of 1980. (Photos by
Cliff Simonton)*

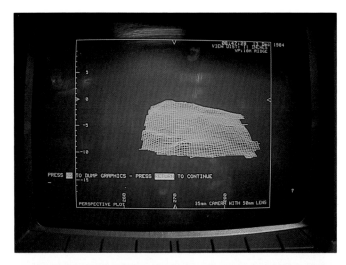

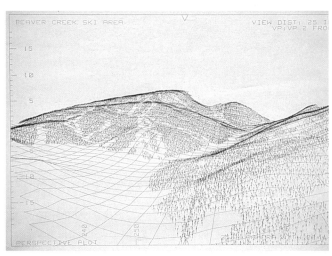

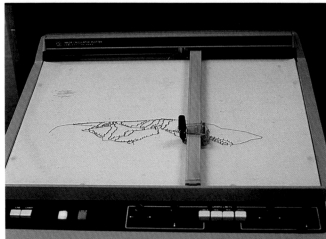

*B*eaver Creek was the first ski area where computer graphics were used to study the visual impact of trail construction. U.S. Forest Service landscape architect Erik Martin developed techniques that enabled planners to determine what the mountain would look like after the ski runs were cut. Trail design information was fed into the computer, which then generated a distorted-square image of the mountain, complete with trees, to give an accurate representation of the visual changes. The computer graphics could be color enhanced as depicted in the painting, below, by Martin. (Photos by Erik Martin)

Beaver Creek a winter sports site. Lucas said he would withhold approval until the state consolidated its position. Governor Vanderhoof asked the land commission to investigate the whole matter further, and Tom Evans finally threw up his hands and said they'd already been investigating it for three full years.

"By the end of 1974," wrote Forester Paul Hauk in *Beaver Creek Ski Area Chronology,* "Vail Associates had spent approximately $6 million on the project and committed themselves beyond the point of no return and with it a hope that they could open for the '77-'78 season. It had been estimated that the interest on the borrowed money earned the United Bank of Denver approximately $425,000 in 1974 alone. Taxes on the land and planning-staff salaries were consuming approximately $35,000 a month while the environmental concerns and socio-economic impacts of the development were being debated and filling space in newspapers all over the state."

The year ended with the Beaver Creek project jackknifed like a truck in a blizzard on Vail Pass.

Just before he left office in January, Governor John Vanderhoof fired the first shot of 1975 by giving state approval to Beaver Creek. The following day the new governor, Richard Lamm, who had initiated the Olympics debate, took office and reversed that decision. Regional Forester William Lucas then designated Beaver Creek as a winter sports site. Governor Lamm appealed the designation. So did the Sierra Club Defense Fund. In Washington, D.C., Colorado Senator Gary Hart asked John McGuire, chief of the Forest Service, to review William Lucas's decision. McGuire ordered a review of everything.

Another year of review, resolve, proposal, and promise began between the county, the state, the Forest Service, and Vail Associates. Finally, on February 20, 1976, a front-page *Denver Post* photograph showed Richard Lamm holding a statement that gave approval to the Beaver Creek project.

At the ground-breaking in July, 1977, Charlie Eaton, pioneer farmer, watched former President Gerald Ford take the first ceremonial scoop of earth out of the valley. Asked that day what he thought of a ski resort in his beloved pioneer home, Charlie shrugged and grinned. "Might as well," he said. "It's all gone to Canadian thistle — you can't farm it."

Ten years later, on the spot where Charlie Eaton had rigged his waterwheel, a village emerged with angled streets and the stone and stucco look of southern Europe. A cavernous underground parking lot swallowed most of the cars allowed in the valley. Air monitoring instruments, calibrated to state standards, tested the air 24 hours a day. Annie Holden's barn, surrounded by million dollar homes, remained intact. Two thousand acres of elk range had been set aside east of the mountain. At the valley entrance, the Howard-Offerson-Nottingham house, still

A High Volume Air Sampler, shown here during a calibration, measures the amount of dust and other airborne particles over a 24-hour period. (Photo by Cliff Simonton)

Clockwise from upper left, Beaver Creek Village at night, the 15th green, the Village Hall, and Turquoise Lake at the headwaters of Beaver Creek.

CLIFF SIMONTON

DAVID LOKEY

CLIFF SIMONTON

KEN REDDING

DAN COFFEY

PETER RUNYON

CLIFF SIMONTON

DAVID LOKEY

DAVID LOKEY

CLIFF SIMONTON

Clockwise from upper left, beautiful home in Beaver Creek, sheep at the valley entrance, wildflowers and wildlife, pioneer house converted to Mirabelle Restaurant, and restoration of the historic Holden Barn.

125

The Great Gift

CLIFF SIMONTON

E very year around mid-October ski area managers begin eyeing the skies to the northwest and wondering how the jet stream will position itself for the following six months.

The yearly undulation of the jet-stream across the western United States is crucial to Colorado's economy since snow storms follow the jet stream and no ski area can get along without snow.

Fragile, ethereal, and oh-so-profitable, the gift of snow begins as grains of sea salt, motes of dust, or particles of bacteria tumble through cold, moist clouds picking up coatings of frozen crystals, each taking its six-sided form from the molecular structure of water. The crystals continue bouncing through the clouds, connecting and assembling themselves into snowflakes, and finally floating down to earth.

There the snowflake goes right on changing, depending on such conditions as wind, temperature, and humidity. The change most appreciated by skiers is called sublimation, whereby snowflakes lose their moisture content directly into the air without going through a liquid stage. They neither melt nor evaporate; in the high, cold Colorado air, they simply dry out, transforming even a relatively moist snowfall into light, fluffy powder overnight.

But moist, heavy snow rarely falls during Colorado ski seasons. Winter storms, born in the Gulf of Alaska, track to the southeast over Washington, Oregon, and northern California, and leave wet snow on the Cascades and the Sierra, where 10 inches of snow are equivalent to one inch of water.

The storms rush across Idaho and northern Utah and into Colorado. There they rise toward the Continental Divide, cooling 3.5 degrees for each 1,000-foot increase in elevation.

The cold, dry air removes even more moisture from the clouds so the snow that finally falls on Vail and Beaver Creek has a 30-to-1 snow-to-water ratio, 4 percent drier than even the famous powder snows of Utah.

Let a foot of those magic, icy crystals fall, and hear the shouts of joy in the Back Bowls. ∎

standing among its pioneer sheds and barns, had been converted into a French restaurant.

Mountain planner Dean Kerkling discovered a computer program used by the Forest Service to judge the visual effects of logging and immediately recognized the benefits of applying computer technology to ski area design. The computer, programmed with trail design information, printed out a detailed picture of the finished mountain, giving planners a chance to correct any design glitches before tree-cutting began. Both deer and elk liked the edge-of-timber habitat created by the new ski runs.

Beaver Creek, its willow-aspen-cottonwood ecosystem intact, still ran high and clear through the village. Tree-cutting in the valley was strictly controlled. "No tree over three inches in diameter, one foot above grade, will be removed without prior approval by the Design Review Board," said a memo. To enforce those regulations, Vail Associates fined contractors $1,500 for each tree that they knocked down by accident.

Ironically, the beavers of Beaver Creek had their own concept of timber management. They could chew through a three-inch tree in less than five minutes. A memo from the environmental officer in the autumn of 1979 addressed that problem: "It is apparent that right smack in the middle of the village project is a colony of beavers arduously stockpiling winter feed. How do you tell a beaver that some aspens are important and should be left alone?" High-tech computer programming helped design the mountain, but it took plain old-fashioned chicken wire, wrapped around the base of aspen trees, to prevent the beavers from doing what came naturally.

Beaver Creek finally opened in December, 1980, but the road to that day had been so long and costly that one reporter called Beaver Creek "The Last Resort."

Former President Gerald Ford and Governor Richard Lamm presided over the ribbon-cutting, and Lamm, in tribute, said: "Like Tiffany's is to jewelry stores, like Gucci is to luggage, like Cadillac is to automobiles, that's what Beaver Creek is going to be to ski areas in this country."

Unfortunately, the weather on dedication day brought back memories of Vail's opening day 18 years earlier as nature once again had the last laugh. Snow conditions, advertised as "good to marginal," were actually marginal to awful. The day after it opened, Beaver Creek closed temporarily for lack of snow.

Ohlsson

THE
FORD
FAMILY

VII

Gerald Ford learned to ski at a farm outside Pittsfield, Massachusetts, where skiers in the 1930s, above, tried out America's new sports craze. Farm owner Clarence Bousquet installed rope tows on the slopes of Yokun Mountain, shown at left in 1937, and used a flock of Dorset sheep to keep the slopes trimmed during the summer. Bousquet invented a rope-tow gripper and also offered the nation's first night skiing in 1936. (Photos Courtesy of Paul Bousquet)

T HE ROAD RUNNING SOUTH out of Eagle, Colorado, angles through pastureland, comfortably green in late summer and spotted with huge cottonwoods leaning over farmhouses. Rain falls steadily out of a gray evening sky. Horses stand patiently under it.

On the left, Steve and Linda Jones's plain log ranch house stands close to the road. Steve runs a string of saddle horses at Beaver Creek; Linda teaches home economics in Eagle. Every August, they throw a lamb roast and pot-luck picnic, a real wing-ding that draws a mixed bag of cowboys, condo owners, resort executives, cops, doctors, construction workers, and ski instructors from every part of Eagle County and a few spots beyond.

As shelter against the rain, Jones has rigged a big, open-sided, striped tent next to the house. A farm wagon topped with boards serves as a table and is crowded with pot-luck offerings of scalloped potatoes, macaroni and cheese, Jello salad, and chocolate cake. A vat of coffee steams at one end.

The rain hasn't kept anyone away. Cars and pickups line the roadside and the crowd spills across the lawn toward the shelter of the tent, everyone talking a mile a minute, catching up on county news. Kids in yellow slickers discover that the rain puddles on the tent top can be released by poking a stick under them. They scream with delight, splashing mud and water. Then someone says quietly, "They're here."

A blue-gray Lincoln Continental pulls up, and Steve and Linda walk out to the driveway to greet President and Mrs. Gerald Ford. The former president carries a bowl of potato salad. Great mounds of sliced roast lamb are now brought to the wagon-table and the feast begins. The Fords take paper plates and find a place in line, passing the time of day with people who amble over to say hello. A few heads turn, but for the most part, the talk in the tent goes on uninterrupted. After all, the Fords have been coming to the Jones's pot-luck lamb roast for years.

Steve met the president in Beaver Creek one summer when the Fords' daughter Susan wanted to give her own daughter a ride on a horse. "So I took a horse up to their house," said Steve, "and while Susan led the horse around, the president and I sat on the curb and visited a little. And Betty came out to talk, too."

Curbside chatting came naturally to the Fords, who fit in comfortably at big events like the American Ski Classic and the World Forum or at small town gatherings like Vail's Fourth of July parade and Christmas tree lighting. Betty Ford took time to dedicate Vail's new library. Gerald Ford, standing on a hay wagon and giving a rousing, all-American speech, dedicated the Schoolhouse Museum in Ford Park.

The association between the Fords and Vail has its roots in the pioneer days of American alpine skiing, a sport that grew popular in the 1930s when good old American inventiveness solved the problem of getting skiers uphill so they could slide back down again. The invention, called a rope tow, used an engine — often from an old Model T — and several hundred feet of rope wrapped around a wheel at the top and bottom of a slope. The rope tow jerked the hapless skier uphill along a rutted, icy groove, burning his hands and taking a heavy toll on his quadriceps and shoulder sockets. He hung on valiantly and released the rope quickly at the top before the wheel grabbed his coat or scarf or any

Gerald Ford and Betty, with three other skiing couples, built this cabin near the slopes of Caberfae Ski Area west of Cadillac, Michigan. (Photo courtesy of W. Anson Hedgecock) Facing page, the Fords on skis, from left: Jack, Susan, Gerald, Steve and Mike.

other part of him left dangling.

"Skiing was hard work in those days," said Gerald Ford, "and those rope tows were tough."

Ford, a law student at Yale, first skied at a small area near Pittsfield, Massachusetts, where a farmer named Clarence Bousquet had noted the glut of weekend skiers sliding around on nearby hills and saw their potential as a winter cash crop. He promptly ran two rope tows up Yokun Mountain, a 600-foot hump of Berkshire County that rose right behind his farm. Skiers came by the hundreds.

Ford tried the slopes of Yokun Mountain as a beginner in 1938. He learned quickly and soon graduated to the longer, steeper runs at ski areas all over New England. Gerald Ford fell in love with skiing, and the romance went on for the next 46 years.

He next skied at Caberfae, Michigan, an area 100 miles north of Grand Rapids, where he practiced law. In 1947, lawyer Gerald Ford met dancer Betty Bloomer, who quickly realized that she had a dyed-in-the-wool skier on her hands. As she later explained, "I figured if I wanted to spend weekends with him, I'd better get myself a pair of skis."

She bought the skis and outfitted herself in the latest ski fashions — baggy gray gabardine pants and a navy blue jacket. "I still have that old jacket," Betty confided. "I loved it. It was long, and it kept my bottom warm." She bought mittens with leather palms to ease the agony of the rope tows and went off to Caberfae where she spent winter weekends learning to ski and getting to know the lawyer from Grand Rapids.

Gerald Ford married Betty Bloomer in October, 1948, just two weeks before Michigan's 5th District elected him to Congress. The Fords moved to Washington, D.C. and days on the slopes at Caberfae were gone forever.

But they still found time to ski weekends at Seven Springs in Pennsylvania and spent Christmas vacations at Boyne Mountain in Michigan. The children — Mike, Jack, Steve, and Susan — all put on skis as youngsters. Every year on the Friday after Thanksgiving, the Ford family marched into a Washington ski shop to outfit themselves for the winter. They traded in whatever equipment couldn't be passed down to the next younger child.

"Poor Susan," murmured Betty. Not only was Susan at the end of the line for leftover equipment, but once, when the Fords arrived at a

133

ski area, they found that Susan's luggage had been left behind, "and that was traumatic for the only little girl in the family."

Betty barely survived the yearly ordeal of getting everyone out the door with all the skis, boots, poles, parkas, pants, goggles, scarves, mittens, and other items needed by a family of six on a ski vacation. At airports, they rented two cars to get themselves and all their equipment to the ski area.

When the children grew up, the Ford family went west to try the big mountains at Sun Valley, Alta, and Park City. In 1968, they skied at Vail and liked it so much that one night they held a family conference in their rented condominium at Manor Vail.

Was this the place? Did they really want to spend all their Christmases in Vail? They all said yes.

"It was a big decision for us and for the kids, too," said Betty. "We were not in a financial situation where we could buy a place outright. We had to borrow money and we borrowed it on our children's life insurance policies. So they were part of it."

The Fords' new condo looked right out over the main street of Vail. They moved into it in 1970, little knowing what a short time they would have to enjoy the peace and quiet there.

In the summer of 1974, the man Vail knew as Jerry Ford, skier, became Gerald R. Ford, the 38th President of the United States.

The president planned to ski at Christmastime and Vail residents wondered where he would stay. It couldn't be at the Lodge condo. It was too central and too hard to secure. Several Vail homeowners, rumor had it, offered their houses at ridiculously high prices. Then Richard Bass, a member of the board of directors of Vail Associates and owner of the Snowbird, Utah, ski area, solved the problem by offering his house at Vail. Perfectly located near the village and the mountain on a road that could be closed off, the Bass house sported the rustic look of a mountain ski chalet with wrought-iron chandeliers, stone fireplaces, and homey furniture made for stretching out after a day on the slopes. Five bedrooms and a downstairs den big enough for meetings gave the Fords all the room they needed. And they could walk to the nearest chairlift.

On December 22, 1974, the Ford family arrived in Vail with a retinue that included house staff, military aids, political advisors, and the Secret Service.

Christmas always meant prime skiing and partying in Vail, and the presence of the First Family made it even more exciting. Helicopters flapped over the valley; limousines glided past security stations set up on Mill Creek Circle. Reporters were everywhere. Every morning they lined up behind the ropes across the street from the Bass house and threw questions at anyone coming out of the house. Did the president have eggs or pancakes for breakfast? Was he going skiing today? What

*V*ail house, owned by Richard Bass,
where the Ford family spent many
vacations during and after their years in
the White House. (Vail Associates Photo)

color sweater was he wearing?

On Christmas Eve, Secret Service agents closely examined the furnace room at the Vail Interfaith Chapel, looked through drawers of Sunday School materials, peered into closets, and scrutinized the whole building. The president and his family arrived for the Christmas Eve service and took seats in the back. The religious and the merely curious pressed into the church, packing the pews and filling the aisles. Hundreds gathered out front. The Rev. Don Simonton, making last minute arrangements at the altar, found himself stranded there by the crowd and had to go outside and around the building to the front door to start the service. But he discovered that the Secret Service had blocked the entry and he had to pound on the door to get in.

Later that night the temperature dropped sharply; by early morning it registered 28 below zero. Jon Moller, caretaker of the Bass house, lived downstairs in an apartment off the den. At 6 a.m. on Christmas Day, Jon went upstairs to make sure everything was in order. He found President Ford eating breakfast alone, with a blanket wrapped around his shoulders. When the two men exchanged Christmas greetings, the air fogged in front of their faces. Startled, Jon looked at the thermometer. It read 46 degrees.

Excusing himself, he hurried down to the boiler room and found the furnace cold as stone. He tried to light it but couldn't. "Now with the president of the United States sitting right above the boiler room, you don't dare mess around too much with matches," said Jon later. Instead, he called a plumber.

Bill Burnett answered the phone with sleep still in his voice. "Merry Christmas, Bill," said Jon. "What the hell's going on?" answered Bill. Jon explained that the Fords were without heat. Bill explained that it was 38 below in Minturn and he probably couldn't get his truck started, but he would try.

In spite of the cold, Bill got to the Bass house, repaired a stuck valve in the furnace, and drank a cup of coffee with Jon as the house gradually warmed up. Pulling on his coat, Bill looked up and saw Gerald Ford walk into the room. "I just wanted to meet the man who'd come out on Christmas morning to fix somebody's furnace," said the president.

Sub-zero weather kept some skiers off the slopes, but not the Fords. Although Betty Ford had given up the sport by that time, the rest of the family still loved it. Even though his presidential duties followed him to Vail, Gerald Ford planned to ski at least part of every day. That meant that the Secret Service went skiing, too.

Seen by the public on city streets, Secret Service agents have generally been viewed as somber guardians with nervous eyes. But they also watched over presidents at play. With some presidents, that meant merely a stroll down the street, a few laps in the pool, or a game of golf. But in recent decades, Secret Service agents have protected sports-minded presidents and vice-presidents in speedboats and sailboats and on horseback.

When Gerald Ford became president of the United States, the Secret Service polled its members to find out how many skied well enough for official duty on the slopes.

A week or so before Christmas, Larry Buendorf, special agent-in-charge of the presidential skiing detail, arrived in town with a handful

137

Ford and friends: with Walter Mondale, facing page, and the Vail Ski Patrol, above. (Vail Associates Photos)

of Secret Service skiers. While other advance agents checked out buildings or the layout of streets, Larry checked out Vail Mountain. He first turned for help to the Vail Ski Patrol, finding a well-trained organization with purposes similar to those of the Secret Service: protection and safety. The ski patrol and Secret Service went together like ham and eggs. "They were the backbone of our organization," said Larry.

Together, they weeded out those Secret Service volunteers "who thought they could ski until they got to the top of the mountain." The survivors honed their skills at the ski school, and then the whole group went out with the patrol to learn the terrain and to build up lung and muscle power needed for work at 11,000 feet. They skied Vail Mountain from east to west and from top to bottom — timing runs the president would use, checking the best routes down to the village, and finding out where the chairlifts went and how to evacuate them. Many a friendship was forged on those cold winter mornings between the Secret Service and the ski patrol.

President Ford's days on the mountain were mapped out well in advance. Snowcats groomed the runs to perfection the night before. The president's party consisted of his ski instructor, Pepi Gramshammer, his physician, Rear Admiral William Lukash (who fell so often that the patrol dubbed him "Crash Lukash"), and family members and friends — all flanked by members of the Secret Service, the ski patrol, and the Vail police.

Each morning the presidential party marched to Chair 16 (now the Vista Bahn) at 10:30 a.m. after the morning crowds and ski classes had dispersed. Although skiers rarely recognized the president on the slopes, they saw him when the party cut through the lift lines. But, as ski

DAVID LOKEY

KRISTA ELRICK

JILL VIG

BARRY STOTT

PETER RUNYON

*E*ach winter, the Fords host the American Ski Classic at Vail and Beaver Creek. The week-long skiing extravaganza includes World Cup races, the Legends of Skiing races and the Jerry Ford Celebrity Cup.

patrolman Chupa Nelson recalled, "He'd stop and shake hands and be very personable. People would call out hello, but it really wasn't that tense. In fact, I think the presidential group had more fun than anyone else on the mountain."

Sometimes the president asked members of the press to ski with him. "There were about seven of them who were good enough," Ford said, "and they were fun because they understood skiing." The president understood skiing, too, and managed to enjoy himself despite a tight schedule and the protective group surrounding him. "I learned to be oblivious to the Secret Service and everyone else," he said, "and just ski."

Occasionally, the group stopped for a picnic at Ski Patrol Headquarters or for lunch at The Cookshack at Mid-Vail, but more often they skied right through the lunch hour and arrived back at the Bass house by 2 p.m.

"We just flowed with the people," said Larry Buendorf, "and we never closed off the mountain. I used to read in the papers, 'They closed off the whole mountain.' We never did that. On press day, we closed off one run for about an hour. Vail Associates would bring up the press by snowcat and put them on the slope in a certain area. They figured if they left the run open, skiers would be crashing into the press. Safer to close the run."

As for Buendorf and his Secret Service detail, their mountain duty hardly qualified as recreational skiing, but it wasn't all bad. "What a refreshing experience, coming out of Washington, D.C., into Vail," said Larry. "The locals took us in and showed us the way of mountain life. It's as if they were saying: 'Relax, you'll find friends here. You don't have to be as stressed as you are in New York or Washington.' And we did relax. They made things comfortable for us."

But for some on Ford's staff Vail's environment seemed strange — a town cut off from civilization by rows of mountain ranges where people talked only of skiing. They shivered and longed for the city.

In 1982, when the American Ski Classic began at Beaver Creek, Gerald Ford tried ski racing for the first time and enjoyed the challenge. But the days of presidential skiing were coming to an end. His left knee, injured in football years earlier, had been re-injured on the slopes and required surgery. Ford weighed his love for skiing against possible permanent knee damage and made his decision. In March, 1984, the president hung up the boards for good. He had been skiing for almost half a century.

"Rest assured, the man is an athlete," said Larry Buendorf. "It's too bad about his knees. He could have gone on skiing for a long, long time."

Instead, Gerald Ford poured his enthusiasm into golf. "I had played on and off infrequently," he said, "but I never really took it up or tried to improve until after I left the White House."

In 1983, the Fords moved into the home they built in Beaver Creek and spent summers, Christmas, and a couple of weeks in early spring in the Vail Valley. Ford's new-found interest in golf resulted in the Jerry Ford Invitational Golf Tournament, a star-studded shindig that raised money for charity each July. As a winter complement, the American Ski Classic featured World Cup competition and races for former Olympi-

In the starting gate at the Jerry Ford Celebrity Cup. America's skiing president took up racing just a few years before knee problems forced him to "hang up the boards." (Vail Associates Photo) Left, the Fords discuss plans, as foundation walls go up for their Beaver Creek home. (Bruce Benedict Photo)

The Fords' involvement in the Vail Valley is year-round and includes summer activities such as the Jerry Ford Invitational Golf Tournament, the World Forum, judging the July 4th parade and performing dedication ceremonies for the town.

DAVID LOKEY

DAVID LOKEY

PETER RUNYON

PETER RUNYON

ans and celebrities.

Ford also invited world leaders who had been in office during his term to The World Forum, a conference on international issues. "This was totally my idea," he said. "I thought it would be good to have something like this in Vail; the former leaders responded and they come every summer."

The golf tournament, the ski classic, and the forum certainly enhanced Vail's reputation, but what really endeared Jerry and Betty Ford to the community went far deeper than merely publicizing the resort. It had something to do with who they were and how they lived and the way they treated people.

Even when the Fords resided in the White House, their casual, informal style often surprised even casual, informal Vail. For example, Vail residents Mike and Ruth Holberg remembered a party given for the Fords by Sheika and Pepi Gramshammer. "I was standing in a group talking to the President," said Mike, "and I kept fumbling with his name. I called him President Ford and then I called him Mr. Ford and then I called him Mr. President. Finally he put out his hand and said 'Why don't you just call me Jerry?'"

In the summer of 1976, Mayor John Dobson and his wife Cissy gave a party to introduce the president to the town council. "The council and their wives arrived on time for once," said Cissy. "And they were all dressed to the nines; the men had on white shirts and neckties and coats. Then President Ford arrived wearing an open-necked golf shirt under his coat. A little later I looked around and noticed that none of the councilmen had neckties on anymore. The following morning when I was tidying up I found a half dozen neckties behind the books in the bookcase or stuffed under chairs and sofa pillows."

Councilman Joe Staufer hoped to introduce his Austrian parents to the president that night. They were staying next door to the Dobsons, but when Joe went to get them they had gone for a walk. "My parents will die when they find out they missed you," Joe told the president. The next day the senior Staufers were startled when a Secret Service agent knocked on their door to say that President Ford was playing golf nearby and would like to meet them. Could they come outside for a chat and have their pictures taken with him?

Betty Ford pleasantly surprised people, too. When her hairdresser, Karl Hovelmann, proudly showed her a picture of his five-year-old granddaughter, Cassandra, Betty told him she would bring Cassandra a Christmas present. "Of course, I knew she was too busy. I didn't expect anything," said Karl. "But here she came on Christmas Eve with a gift for Cassandra. She didn't have someone drop it off; she brought it herself."

One night a young Vail resident named Caroline Thompson was asked to baby-sit for the Fords, who had their granddaughter with them. Caroline, in her early 20s, was fighting a losing battle with cystic fibrosis. When she got to the Fords, they had decided not to go out. Instead of dismissing Caroline, Betty invited her in and soon they were deeply involved in a discussion about cystic fibrosis while Gerald Ford patted the baby to sleep in another room.

"The Fords are just like any other people," observed Steve Jones. "I drop in to see them; I don't see anything unusual about it. I would assume that if they were driving down the road where I live, they might stop in. I wouldn't know why not."

That's just what the Fords do every summer when the Joneses throw their pot-luck lamb roast. Jerry and Betty bring the potato salad.

Mountain

Children

$\blacklozenge$

VIII

Misha Moritz on the race course, above, and the Krueger family in the 1960s, facing page: Ben with Charlie on his back, Bernie, John, and Celine. Ray LeRoy, page 148, tackles the slopes. (Photos by Barry Stott)

A FEW DAYS BEFORE CHRISTMAS of 1962, Guy Parker moved into a room at The Lodge with his parents, his sister, a cat, a dog, a couple of parakeets, a family of gerbils, and a collection of houseplants from their former home in Denver. The family celebrated the season with a tiny Christmas tree propped in the clutter. On Christmas Eve, the pipes froze and burst and flooded the room.

The Parkers endured those cramped and difficult conditions for three weeks while their house was being finished. The Lodge housed many Vail employees, all working frantically to get the resort going. Guy didn't understand what the turmoil was all about, but he never forgot the tension and excitement that permeated the place during Vail's first days.

As a six-year-old, Guy's life was far less hectic. He went to school each morning with six other children in a room at The Lodge, skied most afternoons, and spent evenings at home. Vail offered nothing for children in those days — no playgrounds, clubs, movies, malls, or television.

"I missed television," Guy said. "Not in the sense of wanting it; I think it was good for me not to have it. But there's a gap there, and when I talk to friends who had television, they talk about heroes they had in Westerns and cartoons. These are people I never heard of. Watching television, in this culture, is like being well-read, in a sense. And there's a whole section of that, like a book, that I haven't read.

"I probably spent 30 percent of my time reading," he continued. "There wasn't anything else to do at night. And as far as friends were concerned, it was like a small farming community. The people there were your friends no matter what because you didn't have any choice."

Even Vail adults realized that, in spite of the thrill of resort living, they missed hometown friends and Saturday suppers with parents and grandparents. Although they lived in a mountain paradise, Vail's first residents knew the pangs of loneliness.

Ben and Celine Krueger, for example, dreamed of living in the mountains and could hardly believe their good fortune when they moved to Vail in 1967. But Celine, isolated with her young children in a tiny West Vail neighborhood, found no friends. One day, she drove to Minturn with the children, walked into the hardware store and said to the clerk, "Do you know anyone my children could play with and someone I could talk to?"

Marie-Claire Moritz, a French woman who moved to Vail in 1967 with her Austrian husband, knew all about that far-from-home feeling. "But because we were lonely, we came closer," she said. "We made a little family here with our friends. It was not a standard family — there were no grandmothers — but standards are just things that are made up. Vail was the family. If my kids got stuck in town, Sheika knew

Facing page, children at recess outside the Red Sandstone School, (Photo by David Lokey) and, left, at the Vail Mountain School. The building shown is the renovated Baldauf homestead cabin.

them and gave them a ride home. If they fell off a chairlift, Murphy called me from the ski patrol and looked after them like a father.

"So in the beginning," Marie-Claire said, "there was a melting of different kinds of people — a fusion. I think it made a better breed of young people. They're more sophisticated; you can talk to them about anything. It's because of that mixture. We were all so different to start with."

Schools in Vail and Minturn were short on students, facilities, and programs. Battle Mountain High School fielded a small, brave ski team, with each member competing in all four events — cross-country, slalom, giant slalom, and jumping — because there were not enough of them to specialize. They secretly envied the state's big teams, which were splendidly uniformed and equipped and traveled to races in big comfortable buses. The Battle Mountain team arrived in their parents' station wagons, pulled on homemade black and gold hats — their only official uniform — and went forth to almost certain defeat. "Most of us had old clothes and real junky equipment in those days," said one racer. "But we didn't care. We were mountain kids."

The football team, regularly brutalized by larger, better equipped schools, fared no better. A first-string halfback, who weighed only 118 pounds with his uniform on, said, "I learned to run very fast on that team because I knew if they caught me they'd crush me." Battle Mountain's football team earned the dubious distinction of having the longest losing streak of any team in the state.

But Battle Mountain students cheerfully shared the camaraderie of the perpetual underdog. They didn't win, but at least they got a chance to play. "I certainly never would have played football in a city school," said the halfback, "and I probably wouldn't have been on a ski team either. But those were some of the best years of my life. We just had a wonderful time on those high school teams."

By the 1980s, the ski team had won several state meets and the football team had missed winning a state championship by only a single point. The valley was full of children, and the scene for them had changed considerably. They enjoyed good schools, both public and pri-

vate, a classy town library, an Olympic-sized skating rink, the mixed blessings of television, and more activities than any one child had time for.

Were these mountain children any different from their peers in the city? Peter Abuisi, headmaster at the Vail Mountain School, thought so. He found Vail children gentle, resourceful, and friendlier than children he knew elsewhere. "They do not have the kind of pressure on them that they would have in urban areas, mainly the pressure of crime," he said. "And since they don't have to deal with urban pressures, they are less distracted and more receptive to learning."

But Susan Boyd worried about her children growing up in such a safe and protected environment. She wondered whether they could make it in a city where they weren't known or in a school where they were just one of thousands. Marie-Claire Moritz worried, too. "There's a lack of exposure here to dirt and to the poor," she said. "Everything is so nice and clean. I'm afraid my boys would be lost in the big city."

To meet this parental concern, teachers at Battle Mountain High School arranged a "City Survival Trip." Students, dropped off on Denver street corners, had to get themselves to another location in the city. All of them managed well.

So did Susan Boyd's children when she put them in Denver schools for several years. Her daughter, however, longed for the mountains while one of her sons decided he liked Denver better.

Usually confident and resourceful, Vail children nevertheless suffered some of the adverse effects of resort life and mountain weather. "They feel the transient aspect of the town," said Peter Abuisi. "They see people coming and going all the time. They hardly get to know someone and they're gone. The children speak of this temporary nature of the town with a trace of melancholy.

"And whether they realize it or not, they are sensitive to the seasons and the weather. There's usually a thaw in January, but after that there's much more snow and cold and the long spring storms. Children find that depressing. Children who need extra support need more of it at that time. But with the promise of spring weather in late April and May, they're high as kites."

Many children who grew up in Vail left the valley to try careers elsewhere. Lettie Kuehn, who attended Vail's first school at The Lodge with

JILL VIG PHOTO

156

Raven Idiot

Shortly after the close of the 1983 ski season, a raven, ignoring an entire mountain of trees suitable for nest-building, assembled a mess of twigs on a tiny platform close to the top of Gondola Tower 3. In an effort to discourage such an idiotic choice for a homesite, the gondola crew removed the twigs. Then the men went on vacation.

While they were gone, the raven moved her base of operations to the platform on Tower 1 where she built a large, untidy nest and laid a single egg. By the time the gondola opened for the summer season, a baby raven had broken out of the egg.

The gondola crew named the baby bird Ugly and each morning on their maintenance run they checked to see that Ugly was awake and ready for the day. Mother and chick spent the summer on the gondola platform, gradually turning it white with raven droppings. They seemed unperturbed by the constant procession of gondola cars passing a few feet over the nest, but Mama raven must have decided that one summer of holding open house was enough.

She hasn't been seen since. ∎

DAVID LOKEY

Guy Parker, said: "I went to Aspen after high school and then to Boulder. Then I came back here. I left again and traveled some more, but then I came back. This quiet little valley was the most wonderful place to grow up. And I stay here now because this is my home."

Guy Parker also left Vail several times but kept coming back. He taught skiing and became a ski school supervisor, but that work lasted only six months out of each year. "So here I am with this great job," said Guy, "and then summer comes. Lots of people have adjusted to that twice-yearly change, but I don't like it. There isn't anything very good to do in the summer other than construction. This is my home, and I plan to spend a part of my life here. But every year I say, 'Well, maybe I'll leave.'"

Other children who grew up in Vail also found it a hard habit to break. As one of them put it, "Once you get out and look around, you find there's no place any better."

Jesse Elliot Edeen, whose grandparents pioneered in the valley, loved every minute of growing up in Vail. "I can't imagine living anywhere else," she said, "but I miss the early days. Skiing's a business now, but back then it was a way of life."

Vail children grew up skiing and viewed their mountain as a personal possession. They knew its every bump and hollow, cliff and ridge and secret trail. "My daughter loved that mountain to the very core of her soul," said Susan Boyd.

"The mountain was a playground," added Marie-Claire. "This little Misha of mine, in kindergarten, he was on the mountain with his little cronies. The ski patrol knew them all. Those kids went everywhere, skiing through the trees, skiing like crazy.

"They were brought up on the mountain, and it was a wonderful gift we gave them, something they can come back to."

MOUNTAIN CHILDREN OF AN EARLIER TIME

Vail children on their mountain playground. (Color photos this page by David Lokey)

LITTLE PEOPLE

BRATSKELLAR

SKI CLUB VAIL

Left, two photos, beginner Mike Brown grew up in Vail to become a U.S. Ski Team member. (Color photos this page by David Lokey)

"I enjoy the smallness of Vail, even though it's a little bigger than I like it." John Donovan

married until I could support you."

"That's the closest he ever came to proposing," said Diana. "And right after that he bought the bar. At the ski patrol party that year he got up and announced that we were getting married, and everybody cheered and hurrahed, and I said to myself, 'Oh, that's interesting.'"

They were married in the summer of 1967, with everyone in town at the wedding. When their son John was born in 1970 and the new father walked into the Copper Bar, the local gang stood up and cheered. "Just like Notre Dame had made a touchdown," said John proudly.

Son Matthew came two years later, then daughter Kerry. The Donovans bought a small house on the golf course within walking distance of the bar. John taught skiing every day, served on the town council, and worked in the bar at night while Diana took care of the house, the garden, and the three children. "I was the support force," she said, "the old traditional support force."

The Copper Bar reflected Donovan's personality — nicely weathered, comfortable, and friendly. Old mining tools and a Notre Dame pennant decorated the walls. Construction workers, movie stars, presidents, Charlie's Angels, the ski patrol, and the ski school hung out at the tables.

"It was a nice bar; everybody loved it," said Diana. "Mothers would call and say, 'If you see my son, would you tell him to call home?' It was a message center because everybody was in there. We had fair prices, and we didn't stay open late. It was just a good, clean, fun bar."

One night, the ski patrol came in disgusted because Vail Associates hadn't given them a raise. "Hell, I'll give you a raise," said John, meaning a free glass of beer. Every night after that the ski patrol got a "raise" as soon as they walked in the bar.

Life in Vail worked out well for the Donovans. Then, in 1980, it dealt them a nasty blow.

"I think it was February 8," said Diana, "late in the afternoon. John had his ski school class near the bottom of Chair 11 when some guy shot down Roger's Run, cut above the lift line at high speed and hit him. The doctors said it was like John had hit a tree. He wasn't cut up or anything; there wasn't a sign of injury. But he had a blood clot on his brain.

"They flew him to Denver. A doctor sat down with me and drew some pictures and said we'd have to wait and see. I went outside and cried for a while. John had never been hurt, never been sick, and here he was almost dead. He was in the hospital for two weeks, and the room looked like a mortuary, full of flowers.

"Finally, the doctors said he'd be fine as soon as the blood clot was gone. They let him out on St. Patrick's Day, the day the ski school and ski patrol play their baseball game on skis. John had started that game and always sponsored it and served green beer. So there he was, fresh out of the hospital, refereeing the game. He doesn't even remember it. They never should have let him out so soon. John's OK now. The blood clot is gone, but the scar tissue is still there. It's only slowed him down a little bit."

Donovan resigned from the town council after serving 14 years — longer than any other person. In the fall, he went back to skiing and tending bar. Everything seemed normal.

And then the other shoe fell. The owner of the building where the Copper Bar did business claimed that the Donovans had not maintained it properly and refused to renew their lease.

"We had five more years on that lease, and we felt there were no good reasons not to renew it," Diana recalled. "We fought for it all winter. In the spring, we went to trial and lost the bar on April Fool's Day. When our son, John, came home from school and wanted to know what happened, I said 'We lost the bar.' He said 'You're April Fooling me,' and I said 'No' and he ran into his room and cried and cried. My husband walked into town and took down the bar sign. We'd been open every day for 15 years."

John finds it hard to talk about the bar. "You know, a person who owns something shouldn't say it's great. But it was a great bar. It was a healthy bar, if bars can be healthy. You can't find anyone in this town who would say anything else. So, well, it's gone."

John bought out his partners in a small garbage collection business and named it The Honeywagon. "This may sound foolish," he said, "but I enjoy it. I say it's like getting paid to do your aerobics. And nobody argues with you. If you do your job, your clients leave you alone. If you don't like 'em, just leave their trash and say the hell with it. It's the best business in town."

Reminiscing about his years in town, John said, "Vail's still a great place. You have everything in the world you'd have in a big city right here in a small town, and in 10 minutes' walk you're away from all of it. I enjoy the smallness of Vail, even though it's a little bigger than I like it. But I've changed in the last few years. I like seeing people come, and then I like seeing them leave. October's the best month in the year.

"But it wouldn't take much for me to move. I would hate moving away from all my friends, but I could live some place where the fishing and the hunting are better. I could live where it's a little wilder."

CHRISTIE HOCHTL

Christie Broms, in her first year as Vail ski instructor, learned one day

DAVID LOKEY

"Being outdoors is a wonderful way to spend time with your children, to be together as a family, and to introduce your children to the things you love to do." Christie Hochtl, with family Karl, Karli, and Kevin.

that Austrian instructor Karl Hochtl would be going along to observe her class.

"I was very naive," Christie laughed. "I had no idea he was going along to observe *me,* not my teaching ability."

Karl liked what he saw that day; Christie did too. Raised a world apart, they nevertheless shared the same attitudes toward home and family, along with a passion for mountain living.

Christie grew up in Portland, Oregon, and first skied at Vail in 1966. She graduated from Willamette University, stayed in the state to teach high school and work in a research laboratory, and then, at the urging of a friend, moved to Denver where she worked at the University of Colorado Medical Center.

She liked that job but found the lure of nearby skiing too much to resist. Christie hired on as an instructor at Vail and taught during the Christmas holidays in 1972. "I figured out that I could earn enough to exist on, so I decided to worry about the rest later and just go and have a good time. I met Karl as soon as I moved to Vail."

Karl Hochtl had immigrated to Vail by a route that took him around the globe. Raised in a skiing family in Kufstein, Austria, he knew early in life that he did not want to inherit his father's bootmaking business. At 20, he left Austria for Australia, where the government paid the way of anyone who stayed and worked in the country for two years. Karl stayed five years, working on a railroad and teaching skiing at Parisher Valley.

There he met Roger Staub, who had been hired in 1965 to direct the Vail Ski School. At that time, the ski school insisted that one third of its instructors be European. "Most Americans thought that Europeans were the only ones who knew how to teach skiing," said Christie. "And there may have been an element of truth in that 25 years ago. That's why so many Europeans taught here — because people asked for them. Karl was the first European instructor that Roger brought to Vail."

Karl and Christie married in July, 1975, in an outdoor ceremony in Vail and moved into a Tyrolean-styled house that Karl had built across the valley from Lionshead at Red Sandstone. Sons Karli and Kevin were born in 1976 and 1979.

Without any qualms, Christie traded ski instructing for homemaking. She made curtains, comforters, dustruffles, and clothes for everyone in the family. She baby-sat for friends, taught Sunday School, and volunteered as a teacher's aid at the elementary school. In an era of vanishing homemakers, she seemed an anachronism — a woman out of the 19th century tied to cradle and kitchen.

But Christie found all the freedom she wanted right at home. And when she and Karl planned outings in the mountains, they included the children. "Karli was only three weeks old when we took him along on a hike up Cross Creek, six miles round-trip," she said. "Somehow we always figured a way to take the children.

"It's not easy taking a baby with you when hiking or camping," she added. "It takes forever to get ready and you carry a ton of stuff and sometimes you wonder if it's worth it. But once you get out the door, it's absolutely worth it. It's a wonderful way to spend time with your children, to be together as a family, and to introduce your children to the things you love to do."

Before the boys were three years old, she found tiny skis for them and taught them cross-country skiing. At four, she took them on the mountain for downhill skiing. "They had terrific balance because of the cross-country skiing," she said. "You don't have to teach kids, you just take them along with you and have a good time. And when they wanted to quit, we came home."

Karl rarely has time to ski with Christie and the boys. He teaches private lessons to loyal clients who return year after year to book his time solidly, particularly during February and March, when he often works 35 days in a row. "By the end of March, we're all a little stressed," said Christie.

In the spring, before Karl's construction jobs begin, they relax for a few weeks and visit families in Oregon and Austria. They spend every possible moment camping, hiking, and fishing, and in the fall harvesting wild mushrooms, chokecherries, and rose hips. Karl's hunting trips fill the freezer with deer, elk, and grouse.

The Hochtls manage to live comfortably on Karl's income alone. "But not many people would be happy with the way we live," said Christie. "Some people feel slighted if they can't buy everything they want and put their children in every recreational program in town. But I think it's a disadvantage to try to do everything. If you do, there's no family life and nobody's relaxed."

Christie misses living close to her family but otherwise finds Vail a perfect place to live and to raise children. She might use her teaching certificate when the children grow up, but for now her life as housewife and mother satisfies her completely. "What I do here is important," she said. "Very important."

Her son Karli agrees. "Boy, am I glad you don't work," he told Christie one day. "I'm glad you're here when I come home from school."

TOMMY SHEELY

Tommy Sheely, a teenager from a cramped neighborhood on Chicago's South Side, never forgot his first bus ride from Denver to Vail. A blizzard raged over the mountains and turned a usually pleasant 100-mile trip into a nine-hour ordeal.

But on the way down the west side of Vail Pass, the blizzard suddenly ended. Broken storm clouds drifted low among the cliffs, and shafts of filtered sunlight poured into the valley. "I thought it was the most beautiful place I ever saw," said Tommy, "and I still do."

In 1971, Tommy graduated from college, sank his entire savings — all $600 of it — in a dilapidated Volkswagen van and returned to Vail. Someone stole the van on his first night in town.

The college graduate without wheels found a job cleaning barrooms after hours. He would finish up at three or four in the morning, grab a few hours sleep, and report for his daytime job in a clothing store. In his few spare hours, he tried skiing — going the first time alone and without a lesson or any knowledge of the mountain. After a few wrong turns, he found himself on the nearly perpendicular face of Tourist Trap and had to inch down the entire run on the seat of his pants.

One day, blond, winsome Suzy Robinson walked into the clothing store. Tommy immediately arranged a date. He and Suzy later recalled that it was the worst date either of them had ever had. They tried another date. They fought. Suzy left town, and Tommy knew he'd never see her again.

He left the store, worked in restaurants, bummed around as a house painter, and ended up as a ranchhand west of Vail. One day, out of a clear blue sky, Suzy showed up at the ranch. It was love at second sight.

Suzy found work as a production artist at *The Vail Trail* while Tommy, strictly on a whim, filled out an application with the Vail Police Department. He got the job. "It took a year or two to think of myself as a cop," he said. "In a lot of ways, I still don't think of myself as a cop."

DAVID LOKEY

"I just know I handle life better here in the mountains." Tommy Sheely

Being a cop in Vail meant dealing carefully with offending tourists, many of them doctors, lawyers, politicians, and other professional people not likely to put up with rude or incompetent police officers. "We make some heavy-duty arrests," said Tommy, "but we don't do it the way they do it in Denver or Chicago or New York. We're half police force and half service department. We try to create a small town feeling here.

"One of the difficult things about being a policeman," he continued, "is trying to separate the bad people — the ones who are mean and angry — from the good people who are just caught in a bad situation. If you handle the two alike, you might use too much force with the person who doesn't deserve it and not enough force with the person who does. If you make the wrong choice, you can get hurt."

Tommy took on duties that most small town cops never see: protecting President Gerald Ford, Secretary of State Henry Kissinger, and Jordan's King Hussein.

"Hussein — that was incredible," said Tommy. "He had all his Jordanian Secret Service with him, and we had our Secret Service, State Department personnel, FBI, and our local police. Hussein was staying at the Plaza next to the Vail Village Inn, and I'll tell you, if anything bad had happened, it would have been a real mess with everybody shooting one another.

"As it was, one of his service people started a fire and didn't open the flue and all the fire alarms went off. When the fire department responded and tried to get in, Hussein's Secret Service held them off, and our Secret Service was trying to hold *them* off. It got to be funny."

In July, 1981, Tommy and Suzy were married at the Vail Interfaith Chapel. Since they could not afford to live in Vail, even on their combined incomes, they rented a trailer in Edwards. "It was particularly difficult for me when we lived in that trailer court," said Tommy. "There were nights when I arrested someone and bonded them out, and we both went home to Edwards. I'd wave to them when I was going into my trailer, and they'd wave to me, and I'd wonder if somebody might get drunk some night and slash our tires or try to burn down our trailer. I never really felt secure there."

Bryson Robinson Sheely was born while Tommy and Suzy still lived in Edwards. Just six months later, Bryson was found dead in his crib, a victim of Sudden Infant Death Syndrome. Friends and neighbors overwhelmed the grieving couple with love and comfort. "I was so moved by the support we got from people in Vail that it changed my whole life," said Tommy. "And it changed my attitude toward this town. I could no longer think of it as a place I'd move to one year and might move out of the next — I no longer think that."

Suzy could not return to the trailer. The Sheelys moved west to Gypsum to build a house among the cottonwoods on the Eagle River. Tommy worked four, 10-hour days, but paper work and court appearances often stretched the work week to 60 hours. His schedule rotated every four weeks, from day shift to swing shift to midnight shift. "Going from days to swings is the hardest," he said. "One day I get up at 5 a.m. to go to work, and the next day I'm back home by 5 a.m., trying to get to sleep."

But he found the long, pre-dawn drive home, with the Larry King Show playing on the car radio, a nice way to cool down mentally. Arriving home at 4 a.m., he'd mix himself a rum and Coke and stretch out to watch a rerun of "The Real McCoys." If he got home later, when Suzy was having breakfast, he drank his rum and Coke and chased it with a bowl of cereal.

In 1982, Brittny Cynthia Sheely was born, a beautiful little blond who looked like Tommy. Soon after her birth, two strangers, tormented by the recent loss of their son to Sudden Infant Death Syndrome, showed up at their door. "We wound up talking and crying and reliving the whole thing over again," said Tommy, "and it felt so good to be able to repay somebody with the support that we had when we lost Bryson. We didn't know whether to show Brittny to them or not, but we did and it was OK. And now they have a baby girl. Our stories are identical."

Living in Gypsum means a 74-mile round-trip each workday for the Sheelys, but Tommy prefers it. "I find it a lot easier to live in Gypsum, particularly being a policeman," he said. "It's a different world down here, a different time frame. You don't just drive 37 miles, you go back 10 years.

"But I can't separate my home in Gypsum from Vail or Eagle County. The same river runs through all of it. If I drop a bottle in Gore Creek, it'll end up in front of my house eventually. What happens up there affects what happens down here.

"I just know I handle life better here in the mountains. I always felt swamped in the big city. So many people, so many lines, little aggravations that you don't deal with here.

"Here, I get more out of life."

VICTOR AND CHUS de la LAMA

Although architect Victor de la Lama and his wife, Chus, lived in Mexico City, they were no strangers to skiing. The snow-covered crest of Popocatapetl, fourth highest mountain in North America, rose within sight of the city.

No ski lifts served the mountain, but the de la Lamas and their six children used Victor's snowcat for access to the good corn snow that lay

DAVID LOKEY

"You cannot say that Vail is an average American place, because it isn't. It's like a fairy tale. I think it is a very special place." Chus de la Lama, with Victor.

between 10,000 and 17,000 feet. They could ski the mountain from December to March. The de la Lamas also skied in Switzerland and Canada as well as Sun Valley and Aspen.

In 1962, they saw Vail advertised in a ski magazine and found it instantly appealing — smaller than Aspen and only half as far from Denver. "Vail was an enchanting place, it really was," said Chus. "The mountain so beautifully laid out, the runs fantastic for every kind of skier. And the people were so friendly."

Soon a coterie of de la Lama friends and relatives joined them in Vail. Friends of friends, relatives of relatives, and organized tour groups out of Mexico City followed. "Mexicans were definitely a part of the community of Vail," said Victor, "and good customers for the real estate business."

Victor and Chus made Vail their second home. Their grandchildren attended Vail schools, learned English, and took up skiing. "The children are much freer here," said Chus. "They ride the buses by themselves, shop by themselves. That has been fantastic for them. That they cannot do in Mexico City."

Even before Beaver Creek opened, the de la Lamas toured the mountain by snowcat with Peter Seibert and bought the first lot, choosing the steep, wooded area above the village so that they could ski down to the chairlift in the morning and return home on skis at the end of the day. They designed their home to blend perfectly with the mountain setting, finishing it in 1981. The following year, they celebrated Vail's 20th anniversary, pleased to be included as "founders" of the resort.

Victor and Chus thoroughly enjoyed the relative solitude at Beaver Creek. "Some people like Aspen because there's more action there," said Victor, "but we were not looking for action. We just wanted a quiet vacation." Each year, they spent several months in the valley, finding the summer weather as pleasant as the winter.

During the summer of 1983, however, it rained frequently. In the fall, the snow fell heavily before the ground had a chance to freeze, leaving the soil wet and spongy. Heavy winter storms increased the weight of the snow on the loose, wet ground. In May, usually a cool month, a thaw sent temperatures into the 70s for five days in a row. Sunbathers luxuriated on balconies. But in the mountains, the sudden warmth spelled danger.

The heat penetrated the heavy snows which lay precariously on the steep slopes. The snow melted quickly into the already saturated soil. Weight and the forces of gravity did the rest. In vast areas of Colorado high country, the earth began to move. On May 16, a plane crew, flying over the mountains around Vail, counted more than 75 slides.

One of those slides gathered its deadly forces on a slope 1,000 feet above the de la Lama house in Beaver Creek. Fortunately, Victor and Chus were not in residence at the time. The slope suddenly collapsed and an avalanche of mud and snow plunged into one wing of the house and tore it completely away. On the road below, two Beaver Creek employees barely escaped in their truck. Beyond the path of the avalanche, they turned back to see splintered furniture rolling across the road in a river of mud.

"And to think we picked this location for our house," said Chus sadly, not sure that she could ever go back again.

But aspens and wild flowers have grown over the scarred slope and the de la Lamas rebuilt the house. In spite of the tragedy, they still treasure the fond family memories they had gathered throughout their years in the Colorado mountains.

"You cannot say that Vail is an average American place because it isn't," said Chus. "It's like a fairy tale. I think it is a very special place."

BOB AND EVERETT WARREN

Bob and Everett Warren were born during the 1920s in Red Cliff, Colorado, a town founded by miners and loggers in 1879. Its two-block long main street led to the other end of town and nowhere else. Red Cliff residents liked it that way.

In pre-World War II years, Red Cliff prospered as a busy town of more than 700 people. "We had everything here," said Bob Warren. "Hotels, gas stations, bars, grocery stores — not just one, but several. And a Ford dealership. It was really a nice little town." Bob and Everett returned from wartime service, started a sawmill in 1947, and sold timber to the big mine at nearby Gilman.

In the early 1960s, Red Cliff heard about a new ski area in the Gore Creek Valley but made little of it. As Everett said, "We were conscious of Vail starting, but I don't know if I ever heard anyone make any comment about it." Mining, logging, and railroading supported Red Cliff; its citizens had no use for ski areas.

The sawmill thrived for 20 years, but in 1968 the Warrens had to close it down. "The reason we quit sawmillin' was mainly because we couldn't get help," explained Everett. "We couldn't get enough money for our product to pay the type of wage that other people around was payin'. The Homestake Reservoir projects was actually what started it, 'cause people around here all went to work up there for big money, and we just couldn't get help to keep operating."

Fortunately for the Warrens, Vail Associates needed loggers to cut trails for the new Lionshead area so the brothers took their chainsaw know-how out of the mining town and into the ski area. After a summer and fall of timber-cutting, they were hired to groom snow and worked regular day shifts. However, as more and more skiers crowded the slopes, Vail Associates found it wise to keep skiers and grooming machines apart. The starting time for the day shift was moved back to 4 a.m.

For Bob Warren, that meant getting up at 1:30 a.m. "I don't like to be rushed in the morning," he laughed. Everett stayed in bed until 2. At 3:15, their 4-wheel drive pick-up truck left Red Cliff to follow the high, tight curves of the Battle Mountain shelf road on the 15-mile drive to Vail. At 4, they climbed into the cabs of their grooming machines, crossed the dark, quiet frontage road, and rumbled up Forest Drive onto the mountain to begin the day shift.

For eight hours, Bob and Everett tracked slowly up and down the ski slopes performing their monotonous, yet satisfying tasks. "It's interesting work because of what you can accomplish," explained Bob. "A person, if he wants, can take a machine and go up and down the slopes and leave a big mess, or you can take a machine up there and groom it and

"*A person, if he wants, can take a machine and go up and down the slopes and leave a big mess, or you can take a machine up there and groom it and make it look real nice. If you have any pride in your work, that's what it's all about.*" Bob Warren, standing, with brother Everett.

make it look real nice. If you have any pride in your work, that's what it's all about.''

In 20 years of nights and early mornings on Vail mountain, Bob and Everett saw hares, ermine, bobcats, and coyotes. They watched the dawn light the mountaintop, often a spectacular scene. Bob's wife Ilene sometimes rode the snowcat with him, and one morning, she said, "The sun was just coming up and all the clouds looked like rainbows; it was just one big rainbow."

At noon, the workday ended and the snowcats returned to the barn for servicing. Younger cat drivers grabbed their skis and headed for the mountain to check the slopes they'd just groomed, but the Warren brothers drove back home over Battle Mountain to Red Cliff. They ate dinner at 3:30 and hit the sack between 5:30 and 7 p.m. So went the winter. So went the slow and easy pace of Red Cliff.

Everett planned to retire in 1987; Bob wasn't sure how many more years he'd work. But he and Ilene planned no move to warmer climates when he retired. "Some people are trying to sell their places here because they don't like the winters," said Ilene. "But all our friends are here. Why go someplace where you don't know anybody?"

Although Red Cliff has diminished as a town, Bob and Ilene Warren live contentedly in their log house on the bank of the Eagle River. In the winter, the snow piles up steadily against the side of the old house. "I guess four feet of packed snow would probably be the most we get," said Bob. "But we measure snowfall more or less by the fences — how high the snow is on the fences."

Ilene doesn't mind winter at all. She watches as the snow creeps higher and higher up across her living room window and the steep-pitched roof sheds snow in the same spot. Eventually, snow covers the window completely. "At that point," laughs Ilene, "I just pull the shade and forget about it. It's good insulation."

Snow, distance, and the curves of the Battle Mountain shelf road insulate the old mining town of Red Cliff from the glitter of Vail.

For the Warrens, the separation is distinct and always will be.

BILL BROWN

Idaho native Bill Brown signed up for jump training in Fort Benning, Georgia, during World War II, hoping to join a unit of "para-ski" troopers at Fort Douglas, Utah. But when the para-skiers made their first practice jump, the skis went one way and the troopers another. The army abandoned the concept before Bill ever got out of Georgia.

Brown then requested duty with the 10th Mountain Division ski troopers at Camp Hale in Colorado's Pando Valley. He took the train to Denver where he was delayed for two days while military personnel figured out where Pando was and how to get him there. He spent his first night at Camp Hale sleeping in a mule barn.

Brown fought with the 10th on Riva Ridge in Italy. Badly injured just a few days before the war ended, he spent months in a hospital and finally returned to his hometown of McCall, Idaho, with a medical discharge. While recuperating there, he coached the local ski team and started the Junior National Championships. He returned to the Army in 1948, fought in Korea, was wounded again and barely got out alive. The Army considered him 40 percent disabled. He still carried three pieces of shrapnel in his chest.

But Brown stayed in the Army, served in Austria and Alaska, and was teaching mountaineering skills for the Dartmouth ROTC when he received a letter from Peter Seibert offering him a job at Vail. A return to Colorado mountains appealed to Bill, but so did the Army and the job at Dartmouth. A few years later, however, he decided in favor of Colorado. "I liked the Army," he said. "But I'd been hit too many times, and they didn't want me to go back into combat. So I decided to get out."

In February, 1966, Bill Brown settled down in Vail to oversee the development of Vail Mountain. He managed the construction of trails and lifts at Golden Peak and at Lionshead. His official title changed to

Manager and Director of Mountain Operations. Having visited and worked at ski areas all over the world, Bill brought to his job a definite philosophy of how to build a mountain right, particularly when it came to cutting ski trails.

"I stood alone on the whole thing when I started," he explained. "They used to just cut the trees and leave the stumps. But my philosophy was to build a trail for the least amount of snow. Put bulldozers on the slopes and take out rocks and stumps and bury them in holes and hollows. Build a trail where everybody can have fun, where beginners and intermediates can look 10 feet tall."

The Forest Service and the Division of Wildlife worried that cutting ski trails would cause erosion and that human activity would scare off game. Bill challenged both agencies. He sought advice on revegetation at Colorado State University, experimented with dozens of high-altitude grasses at Mid-Vail, pushed through his own methods of using straw mulch, seed, and fertilizer, and watched the grass grow tall.

"They told me there'd be landslides up there, but 20 years later those trees are as solid as ever," he explained. "They said there'd be no wild-life. Now there's so much game up there the Forest Service wants to

"My philosophy was to build a trail for the least amount of snow . . . build a trail where everybody can have fun, where beginners and intermediates can look 10 feet tall." Bill Brown

have an open season at both Vail and Beaver Creek. It's a known fact — we don't harm the game at all."

Bill also turned his innovative talents to grooming snow, a top priority at any ski area since well-groomed slopes prevented skier accidents. For 18 hours each day of the ski season, 10 to 12 snowcats roamed the face of Vail Mountain. The machines cost upwards of $150,000 each, and many of their design features were born out of conversations between Brown and his crews and passed on to the Logan Manufacturing Company, which built the snowcats.

Brown and his men could take credit for the safety glass, heated windshields, shoulder harnesses, and adjustable seats in the cabs, the variable speed transmissions, the compactor bars on the back of the cats, the wings that operated 12 ways on each end of the front blade, and the design of the tiller, a spiked roller used on hard snow.

"One thing about Bill Brown, he sure takes care of his crews," said snowcat driver Bob Nichols. "He gives us what we need to have a first-class grooming outfit.

"And everybody's encouraged to ski the slopes they've groomed," Nichols added. "That's how you learn what's wrong with your grooming. And if you don't do good — well, for one thing, Bill Brown will come by and tell you. He gets up here and skis. And he doesn't put up with any nonsense."

Brown's job on the mountain covers far more than grooming in the winter and trail maintenance in the summer. "Spring is brutal," he said. "There's nothing worse than spring in a ski area, I don't care where in the world it is. Spring is dirty, the weather's bad, the snow melts, the trash is showing, everybody's tired and crabby, and we have to go right back to work the day after the lifts close because just about everything you see on the mountain that isn't permanent has to come down."

Each spring, on Vail and Beaver Creek Mountains, Brown's crew takes down 400 miles of maze and boundary rope, close to 500 post and tower pads, all the temporary signs, the timing devices on the race course, the seats on all the chairs, and the pads on all the seats. They clean, inspect, and repair the equipment, replace 10 to 20 percent of it each year, and put everything in storage.

"The day after the mountain closes, we start plowing the roads open so we can get trucks up there for water control," said Bill. "We cut water bars into the snow, and if it's warm, we have people up there all night to make sure the water stays in the bars and doesn't wash out the roads or get down into town. That's seven days a week until the snow melts. And maintenance on the lifts starts immediately and goes on all summer. If we have lift construction — and we almost always do — we have three and a half months to do 12 months of construction.

"And then," he added, shaking his head wearily, "we collect trash. Tons and tons and tons of trash. I have people go down the slopes and under the lifts, picking it up. It costs us between $25,000 and $50,000 a year to clean up the trash that people throw down.

"Then the fall comes, and everything we took down in the spring we start putting back up again, getting ready to open on Thanksgiving."

Through the years, Bill Brown has devoted himself to the improvement of Vail Mountain and has done it the way he thought best — often in opposition to agencies, individuals, and even his own fellow managers at Vail.

"You have to have been in the army to understand how Bill Brown operates," said Bob Dorf, former ski school director. "Bill is the epitome of the first sergeant. Sergeants always acted with complete deference to officers, who gave orders as to how they thought things should be done. Sergeants then went out and did those things the way they had to be done.

"At Vail Associates, there were always new officers coming in. Sarge Brown would sit quietly with them in meetings, listen politely to their orders, and then go out and do the job as he saw fit. And 99 times out of 100, he was right."

VIRGINIA PYKE

Virginia Pyke, a California native, supported her husband through college and three years of Presbyterian seminary and moved to Colorado's high country in 1969 when his Denver church suggested that he take time off from big city pressures to serve a church in the mining town of Minturn.

In a fierce October snowstorm, the Pykes and their three children moved into a tiny, two-bedroom house on Minturn's main street. "We didn't know a soul up here," said Virginia. "Jimmy was two years old, Dick was eight, Patty was 10. Dick had to sleep in the dining room."

The following fall she found a teaching job at Vail's elementary school, which held classes in the sunny, carpeted room over the medical clinic. "It was like one big family there," she said. "We'd take the kids sleigh-riding through town singing Christmas carols. And since we got out at 2:30 and had no PE, we could change our clothes and go take a

"Then the summertime comes, and it makes me very aware of just how much I love it here." Virginia Pyke

couple of runs on Bear Tree after school. The kids went too. I loved that school."

But at home, Virginia faced a serious problem — a marriage on the rocks. "We had been having problems because of the church before we came up here," she explained. "Then it all came to a head, we made a decision, and that was it. I had to go on with my life. So I took the three kids with me and pulled out." Her divorce was final in 1972.

She rented a condominium in Vail and took on an extra job as hostess at a restaurant. She managed a few after-school hours with her children; then daughter Patty took care of the younger brothers while Virginia went to work.

High rents and a growing family forced her to move often, always trying to find a decent place to raise three children on her teacher-hostess salary. "It wasn't like I could rent a room and share expenses," she said. "I had my three kids. It was hard."

To save rent, she moved her family to a trailer park in Edwards, 14

A Necktie Party at Vail

Most people know Gore-Tex as a high tech sports-world fabric, a microporous material that can discriminate between water as a vapor and water as a liquid. It breathes but is waterproof — great stuff for tents, sleeping bags, and jackets.

But before Gore-Tex was known in the sporting world, it was used in the operating room. The medical use of the miracle fabric began as a direct result of a conversation on a winter evening in 1971 at a dinner party in Vail.

Ben Eiseman, MD, and William Gore, after skiing together that day, had been invited for dinner at Janet Boyd's home. Gore appeared for the occasion wearing a silky white necktie. Standing at the kitchen bar, he startled his friends by pouring catsup on the necktie. He washed off the catsup, leaving neither stain nor water mark, then pulled from his pocket a piece of the same material, cupped it in his hand, and filled it with water, which it held. Next, he lit a match, held the material in front of it, and blew out the match through the material.

Gore, a chemist who had been part of the team that developed Teflon at E.I. DuPont De Nemours and Co. and who had left to start his own company, explained that the fabric — polytetraflouroethylene (PTFE) — was an expanded type of Teflon that he had recently developed.

Ben Eiseman was impressed. A surgeon at the University Hospital of Colorado, he had been looking for a membrane fabric to use as a blood oxygenator during heart surgery. He was also interested in finding a material suitable for artificial veins and arteries. William Gore's necktie, it seemed, held fascinating possibilities. That evening began the cooperative research between Ben Eiseman and the W.L. Gore Associates, Inc. laboratories.

Although he later refused any credit for the explosion of Gore-Tex in the sportsfield, Eiseman did suggest to Gore at the dinner party that the material might be perfect for rain gear and tents.

In any event, Gore-Tex arteries are as standard today as Gore-Tex sleeping bags. ■

miles west of Vail. "We moved to the trailer in the middle of winter," said Virginia. "Nice as it was, I didn't like living in a trailer. I just don't like that feeling. The kids didn't like it either. And the drive home after work on icy roads was awful. One night, I did a 360 in the middle of the highway. That year was horrendous." Son Dick, having troubles in school and with friends, left home to live with his father.

In spite of her problems, Virginia never seriously considered leaving. Her mother had died while Virginia lived in Minturn; she had no other living relatives, no home in California to return to.

And although they consumed all her time, she loved her jobs. "They're so diverse, that's one reason I make it through," she said. "I love meeting those people at the restaurant, especially the ones who keep coming back year after year. And at school, I get so involved with those little kids, it's like I'm in a completely different world. I don't have to pretend, I don't have to be something I'm not. I can grow with those kids and love them and have fun with them. That's been my saving grace.

"Still," she added, "the winters are awfully long."

Summer always brought a breathing spell — warm weather, dry roads, only one job to contend with. In the summer of 1977, daughter Patty, then 18, found a job in a Vail restaurant. On August 30, Virginia began another year of teaching in the elementary school's brand-new facilities at Red Sandstone.

That night Patty left the restaurant and stopped to see some friends in Avon. She left their place late and pulled onto the highway for the last five-mile stretch home. She never made it. For some unknown reason, her car swerved off the road. Patty died in the crash.

"She just went off the road," said Virginia. "They found no trace of drugs. She might have swerved to miss an animal — we'll never know. She just went off the road. I never went back to that trailer again."

She and Jimmy moved back to Vail — first to a friend's condominium, then to a tiny, one-bedroom place behind Safeway. Jimmy slept on a sofa bed in the living room; when he grew too big for that, he rolled out his sleeping bag on the floor. Virginia buried herself in her work. She had no time to socialize.

Up at 6 each morning, she got Jimmy off to school and herself to Red Sandstone by 7:30. That gave her an hour and a half to plan the day's classes before the children arrived. At 4 p.m., she left school and went immediately to the restaurant where she kept a change of clothes. For the next six or seven hours, she answered the phone, welcomed and seated dinner guests, and kept the restaurant running smoothly. Her day ended at 11 p.m. She treasured Sunday, her only day off.

In 1980, Virginia and Jimmy moved to a new apartment at Pitkin Creek just east of town. Jimmy, a talented and popular teenager, starred in the school's production of "Fiddler on the Roof" during his senior year. "I'm very proud of him," said Virginia. "He's a very strong person.

"And I'm pretty strong myself," she continued. "I've been able to pick up the pieces and move on. But I had to do it on my own. I didn't have anyone.

"Vail is my home; I have roots here. This is where I raised Jimmy. But because I work so much and don't ski, I can't enjoy the recreational part of it, and I kind of dread the winters.

"But then the summertime comes, and it makes me very aware of just how much I love it here."

MIKE AND RUTH HOLBERG

"I've only met one person in my life who didn't like Vail," said Mike Holberg of Dallas," and I'm ashamed to say he's a Texan."

Mike, a manufacturer's representative who called Vail his second home, could not understand anyone who didn't love Vail as much as he did. Holberg just wished he'd known about Vail back in the late 1950s, when he and several friends from Texas sank $15,000 each in Wolf Creek Pass, a ski area buried in the San Juan Mountains. They earned nothing but experience from it. "I lost my shirt at Wolf Creek before Vail ever got started," said Mike.

He did not, however, lose his love for skiing. He had learned how at college in California and the bug had bitten hard. Wanting to share the joy of the sport with wife Ruth and daughter Kris, he took them on a ski vacation to Santa Fe, New Mexico. Ruth hated it. "It was cold," she said, "and I didn't care if I never saw another ski mountain."

Eight years passed before she changed her mind. Meanwhile, Vail had opened and one of Ruth's friends bought a condominium there. In 1967, she invited Ruth to visit. That's how Ruth got back into skiing.

"It was a ladies' trip," she explained, "and it sounded like fun to me. Three of the group had never been on skis before, and one was so scared of heights that when we went to Mid-Vail on the gondola she threw up. Our instructor, Grant Teeple, met us each morning, but he could never get us up to the top of the poma all together to give us a lesson. We just laughed ourselves silly. We had a ball. When I went home and told Mike about it, he couldn't wait to get here. He'd never been to Vail."

Mike took quick advantage of Ruth's new interest in skiing. The family spent Easter in Vail and returned the following December, and again the next spring. "It was a family place," said Ruth. "We heard about Aspen, but we heard that Vail was safer, better taken care of, and better groomed. So we came to Vail and immediately had a good time."

In June, 1969, Mike, on business in Denver, called Ruth in Dallas. "I've got reservations for you on a plane at 8 tomorrow morning," he said. "We're going to Vail to buy a place."

"I thought he'd lost his mind," said Ruth. "We only skied there three times. But Mike loved it, and he said that skiing was the only thing we did together as a family. So we drove into Vail, and it was raining and everything was mud and that night it snowed. You know how June can be. We bought a place at the Christiania. I thought we'd never use it in the summertime. When we came back in July, I was going to stay two weeks. I stayed six. Now summers are what I like best of all."

Summer or winter, the Holbergs found plenty of Texas compadres in Vail. In the summertime, the flatlanders gratefully exchanged the city heat for Vail's cool mountains. Used to traveling long distances in Texas, the drive to Vail seemed just a hop away. They called it "instant Europe." And in the spirit of family fun, Texans just naturally took to skiing. Every major city in Texas had a ski club with membership running in the hundreds. "I understand they even have a ski club out in Muleshoe, Texas," said Mike. "But don't quote me on that."

Vail welcomed the good-time, free-spending Texans with open arms. "The nice thing about Texans is that they're not arrogant and they don't show off," said restaurant owner Marie-Claire Moritz. "They're honest and genuine and they love Vail. And they love our restaurants."

"We're amazed at the quality of the food served here," said Ruth. "When we first came to Vail, Dallas had few good restaurants. But here it was wonderful food, served elegantly in a casual atmosphere. Texans hadn't been exposed to that. You could go in your ski clothes. Mike just loved to come to Vail and not have to wear a tie and coat."

"Even when I was a little boy, my mother put a tie on me," explained Mike. "I never went to church without a tie until I came to Vail." One night, the Holbergs were invited to a party for President and Mrs. Gerald Ford. Ruth strongly suggested that Mike wear a tie. "Why should I?" asked Mike. "He never does." Ruth later laughed about it. "There we were at a big Vail party, and Mike and the president were the only two men without ties."

Mike Holberg's second investment in Colorado ski country couldn't have made him happier. Ruth spends almost six months a year in Vail, and Mike as much time as business allows.

"We're really entrenched in Vail," said Ruth. "And what I love about it is that people are very friendly here, but no one tries to impress anyone. If you go to a party in a big city, you'll notice that people want other people to know who they are. In Vail, they don't care. No one cares — in a nice way. I mean, they're interested in you as a person, but they could care less if you have money. Which is wonderful."

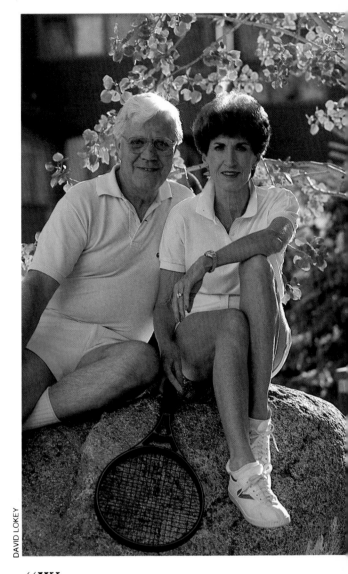

DAVID LOKEY

"*We're really entrenched in Vail, and what I love about it is that people are very friendly here, but no one tries to impress anyone.*" Ruth Holberg, with Mike.

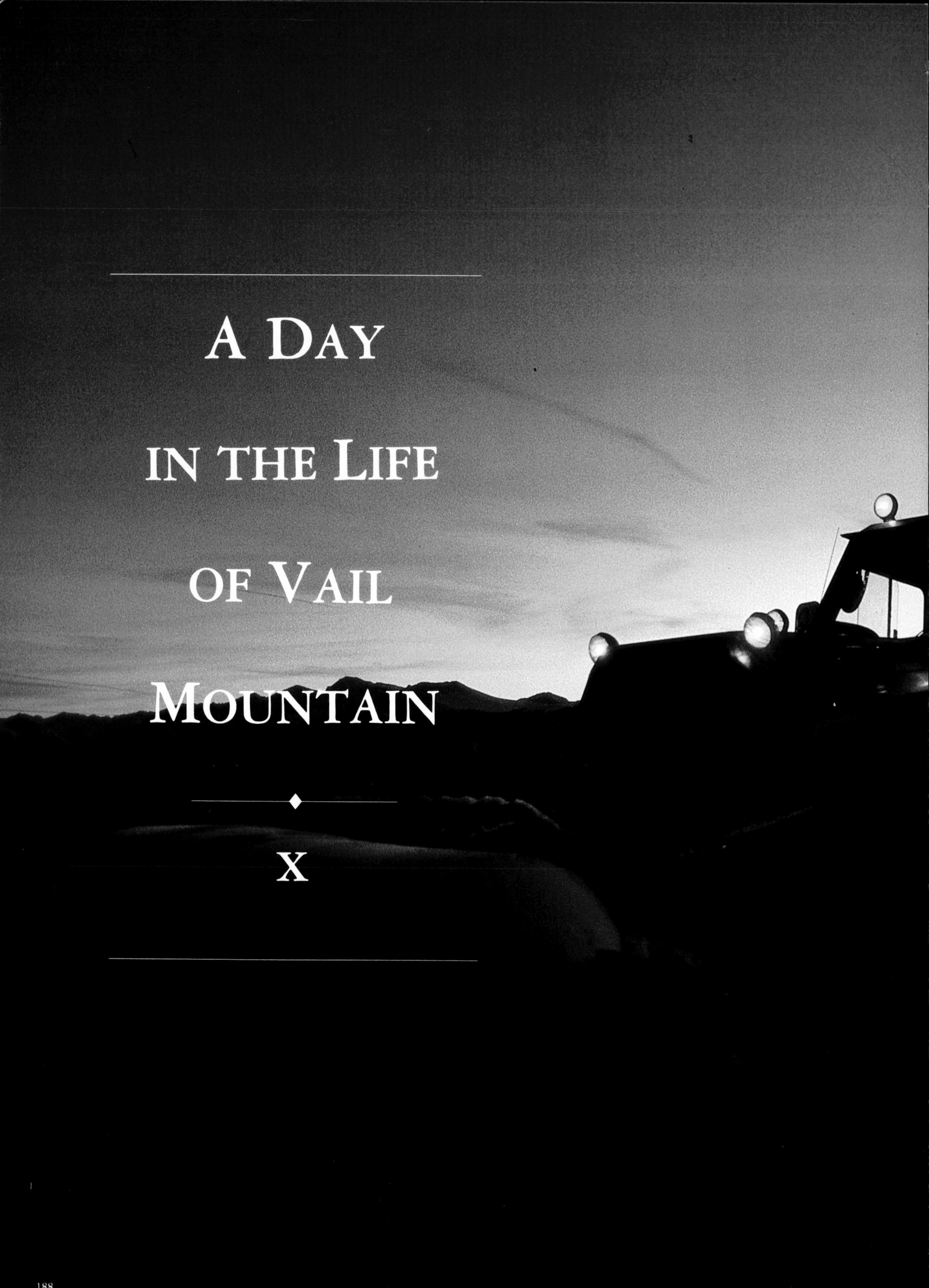

A Day
in the Life
of Vail
Mountain

◆

X

Photographer David Lokey, who spent days and nights on Vail Mountain, captures on film the essence of what goes on there during a 24-hour period. The following pages illustrate his journey.

Like many modern ski resorts, Vail covers its lower slopes and heavy traffic areas with man-made snow. A system of pumps, compressors, and underground pipes convey pressurized air and water to above-ground flexible hoses and portable snowmaking guns. The kind of snow created depends on the air-to-water ratio, which is adjusted according to the outside air temperature.

E VERY DAY DURING THE WINTER SEASON, thousands of skiers pour onto the slopes of Vail Mountain and engage in what the message on the back of their tickets warns is a "hazardous sport." A high percentage of these skiers know nothing of the mountain's dangers — its chill factors, blizzards, cliffs, or burning sun. Many of them know little about their own ski equipment and even less about the technique of skiing itself.

Yet they return at day's end — happy, well-fed, and usually in one piece. They shower, toast the day with a cold beer or a dry martini, order steak tartare, shrimp scampi, and hit the sack.

But a day on Vail Mountain never really ends. A force of more than 2,000, working in shifts around the clock, ensures the safety and well-being of visiting skiers. The ski patrol, ski instructors, mountain hosts, and lift operators are highly visible because they're on the mountain and wear uniforms. But others work behind the scenes, cooking, cleaning, and maintaining equipment. Their work goes on 24 hours a day.

For 18 of those hours, snow cats level, pack, and smooth acres of snow. And while the snow groomers work on the mountain, the lights burn all night long in the 10,000 square-foot central kitchen at Beaver Creek.

Vail Associates' food service, one of the largest in Colorado, employs 500 men and women who work in overlapping shifts. During the ski season, they prepare 250,000 hamburgers, 50,000 hot dogs, and 40,000 bratwurst as well as hundreds of gallons of chili, stew, and soup — all of it transported by gondola to Eagle's Nest and by snowcat to the

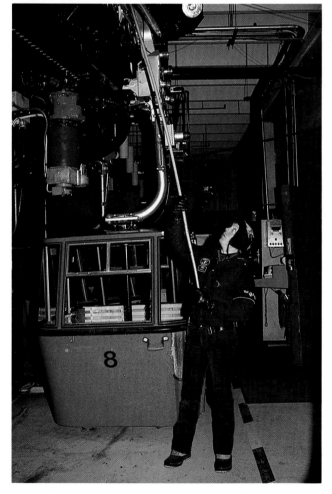

*T*he operation of Vail's gondola requires a two-hour inspection every morning. The 100-ton counterweight, which assures proper tension on the gondola cables, gets a going-over, along with the car launcher, left, checked manually before the gondola opens for the day. Operator in the main control room at Eagle's Nest, above, monitors all gondola systems.

Gondola freight cars and snowcats carry food and supplies to locations on the mountain, while, hours ahead of hungry skiers, food service people prepare for the day.

mountain restaurants. In one ski season, 750 tons of food travel up the mountain and 100 tons of garbage travel back down.

Capable of producing 25,000 skier meals a day, the food service has also served a private picnic at a remote mountain cabin for Jordan's King Hussein, with the lobster bisque, china, crystal, linen, and fresh flowers all delivered to the site by snowcat and skis.

Early each morning, a truck delivers 8,000 pounds of food, packed in steel bins, to Lionshead. The gondola crew loads the bins onto freight cars for shipment up the mountain at 6:30 a.m. Then they begin the daily two-hour inspection of the gondola system.

The mechanic in charge inspects the cables, counterweights, and tracks. After conducting a dry run to check the launching system, he calls out to a crew member, "Let's crank it up." The bull wheels turn slowly and the crew pulls the first cars onto the track. The mechanic and three other employees enter one of the cars and swing out of the terminal. As the car approaches each support tower, the mechanic radios the terminal: "Slow down, please." He carefully inspects every tower, checks all the workings at the Eagle's Nest terminal, and rides back down the mountain. He refers to his morning routine as "doing a lap in the office."

It's 7 a.m. at Eagle's Nest as two crewmen unload the food bins and push them out onto a back deck where a haul cat waits to begin the daily deliveries.

Down in the village, lift operators, ticket checkers, mountain hosts, and members of the ski patrol file into the locker rooms underneath the ticket office. They stretch, yawn, sip coffee out of styrofoam cups, listen to orders for the day, and make notes on snow conditions, weather forecasts, and grooming reports. They pull on uniforms and finish their coffee.

A mechanic crawls up into the labyrinth of the Vista Bahn's inner workings for morning inspection as the mountain workers, their shoulders hunched against the cold, file out of the locker rooms. They board the first chairs of the Vista Bahn and move up the silent mountain.

At 8 a.m., the ticket offices open. Ski instructors converge on their locker rooms, flocks of skiers stamp across the cold, squeaky snow, and the hum of a thousand conversations rises. The sun tops the ridge and floods the scene with light and color.

Ticket checkers note a few oddities of the day as they open the mazes

*S*ki school supervisors and instructors
gather before classes begin. Ticket checkers,
above left, and mountain hosts, above,
receive assignments for the day. Ski patrol
members, left, at their morning "laugh-
in" discuss weather and snow conditions
affecting skier safety on the mountain.

*L*ove and patience are often required when it comes to teaching young skiers. "And this is what it feels like when your skis are in a wedge," explains an instructor, above right, as a class of never-ever skiers learns what to expect before they hit the slopes.

and welcome the crowd. One woman has put the ticket wire through the hole in her earlobe; her lift ticket hangs right there at face level. A middle-aged man wears his boots on the wrong feet, buckles to the inside. Chairlifts scoop up skiers steadily. By 10 a.m., the village is quiet again.

On the mountain, hundreds of employees man the lift shacks, kitchen counters, ski school desks, and patrol rooms. Phones ring constantly. A lift crewman gets word of an electrical failure on Chair 3; the patrol gets its first call from a beginner lost at the bottom of Bear Tree. "Keep going, you're almost to the village," they tell him. A skier, soon to be vacationing in Vail, calls the ticket office from North Carolina and asks whether it will be snowing a week from the following Wednesday. A sink clogs at Mid-Vail. Several ski patrolmen check a possible avalanche site near Apres-Vous. The lift operator at Chair 4 posts the first trivia question of the day: "What's the second highest mountain in the world?"

The haul-cat rumbles across Eagle's Nest Ridge on its third trip of the morning, this time dragging a giant water drum to replenish the supply at Far East restaurant. On his return trip, the driver picks up yesterday's trash at Wildwood.

A mountain host peers over the shoulder of a young woman who can't read her trail map. "That's a trail map from Aspen," explains the host. "Here, let me give you one for Vail." A ski patrolman, empty sled bouncing behind him, swoops into Lodgepole Gulch to pick up the day's first "wreck," a man with a dislocated shoulder.

Chair 9 stops briefly while the operator retrieves a dropped ski pole.

Central reservations provides an important service to people wishing to stay in the Vail Valley's many lodges. Occupancy levels are helpful in forecasting how busy the mountain will be on a given day.

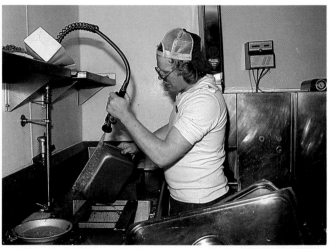

Mountaintop concessions offer quick snacks, as well as hats, gloves, goggles, and suntan lotion. At lunchtime, it's burgers and fries for many skiers, while others visit The Cookshack at Mid-Vail for gourmet dining with a great view. In either case, someone has to clean up afterwards.

A crowd enjoys the sunshine at Mid-Vail. Employees remove a dangerous accumulation of snow from the restaurant roof, chairlift operators keep smiling, and the Vista Bahn gives skiers speedy rides back up the mountain for another run.

*M*ore than 50 strong-skiing, emergency medical technicians staff the professional ski patrol on Vail Mountain. Their central concern is skier safety. At the scene of a "10-50" (accident), patrolmen prepare the toboggan to evacuate an injured skier. "Running the rig," above right, a patrolman uses the side-slip to control the speed of the toboggan. Vail Associates supervisory staff, right, stay in touch with conditions on the mountain to anticipate problems before they happen.

The problem at Chair 3 is fixed, but a plumber still mutters angrily over the sink at Mid-Vail. A ski-school class of five-year-olds lines a bench at Eagle's Nest for a hot chocolate break. One of them weeps, "I want my m-m-mother." The instructor pats her gently and sips his chocolate.

Ski patrolmen set explosive charges on a huge cornice overhanging one of the bowls that is closed to skiing. The patrolmen working along the outer edge of the cornice are on rope belays held by men "dug in" on solid snow.

A man from Atlanta, Georgia, celebrates his 60th birthday in the Nastar gates on Hunky Dory and skis off with a bronze medal. Under Chair 15, a small child follows the blue jacket of the wrong ski instructor and ends up on Columbine in the wrong class. At patrol headquarters, a patrolman advises a woman with sore ankles to buy donuts and put them in her boots. The woman does not understand that he means foam rubber donuts.

A skier reports a ski lost in the Back Bowls; another reports his wife lost on the Meadows. A ski school supervisor finds the misplaced child and returns him to the proper class. At Chair 4, in response to the trivia question, a skier asks: "Is it Lhotse?" The lift operator answers, "No — look at your skis." "Ah," says the skier, "K-2!" The patrol picks up a boy with a wrenched knee on Northstar.

The Mid-Vail restaurant vibrates with the noontime stomp of ski boots. The vice-president of Vail Associates, under a familiarization plan for department heads, is cooking hamburgers on this particular day. At Eagle's Nest cafeteria, the lady with sore ankles purchases four sugar donuts and places them in her boots. A man shyly approaches a

Vail's "highest" resident, at his 11,250-foot-elevation home at ski patrol headquarters on Vail Mountain. A patrolman, above, working in a blast-proof blockhouse, prepares explosive charges for use in avalanche control.

"There's No Comparison."

*T*he Vail/Beaver Creek Ski School, one of the largest in the world, employs more than 650 ski instructors. It provides classes for every age and level of skier as well as programs like "Meet The Mountain," an interpretive tour. Below, a young skier gets pointer from a Ski Club Vail coach on the race hill at Golden Peak. The Club's 12 coaches provide instruction to 150 athletes each year, ages 6 to 20. Established by Vail founder Peter Seibert, Ski Club Vail has produced many all-American college skiers and U.S. Ski Team members.

mountain host to ask if it's true that moguls are made out of haystacks. He doesn't think so.

High above the Back Bowls, where the patrolmen are setting the charges, the cornice — 15 feet thick and 200 yards long — breaks off suddenly, and one of the patrolmen goes down with it. Stopped by the belay rope, he dangles above tons of crashing snow. Patrolmen pull him to safety. At Wildwood, 47 skiers gather for a Meet the Mountain tour. A toddlers' class at Eagle's Nest begins its afternoon-long descent of Simba.

The Chair 4 operator posts a new trivia question: "Who won the Super Bowl in 1973?" The lady with sore ankles returns to complain to the ski patrolman, who later sighed, "I knew what had happened when I saw the sugar all over her socks."

The sun slants, the air cools, and shadows fall across portions of the runs. At 3 p.m., restaurant managers call in requisitions for the following day. Ski patrolmen read assignments for the afternoon sweep; mountain hosts set up fences and take up stations to control speeding skiers. At 3:30, operators close the lifts and shoo off skiers who beg, "Listen, I have to get back to the top of this lift — my aunt's waiting for me up there." The operators smooth the mazes, repair the snow ramps, and pick up trash.

Skiers descend the mountain in flocks. Mountain hosts wave Day-Glo orange poles at speedsters and shout, "Slow down, please. Slow down!"

The ski patrol slowly sweeps the runs, pausing occasionally to call out, "Clearing!" Outside Mid-Vail, food service employees grab their skis

Mountain hosts at control fences caution skiers to slow down as late afternoon skiers crowd the lower slopes.

The skier day ends, but the work goes on as the ski patrol reviews "sweep" assignments, mechanics make repairs within the folds of a snowcat track, windows are washed, money is counted, and a small army attacks the big job of cleaning up.

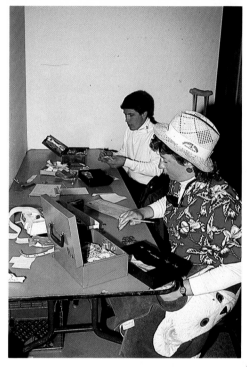

for their single, crazy run of the day. The patrol clears the last of the lower runs and heads for the locker room.

The slopes are empty and silent, but the day is not over. Snowcat drivers climb into their cabs and head up the hill for the night's work. Clean-up crews with buckets, mops, and brushes go to work in the restaurants and rest rooms. In the central kitchen, bakers roll out dough; prep cooks chop up meat and vegetables for tomorrow's stews. The hot food chefs sign on at midnight.

And all night long, the snowcats track methodically over the slopes, smoothing the snow for another day in the life of Vail Mountain.

EPILOGUE

All the Changing Scenes and Seasons

From a meadow high on the north side of the valley, you can see all the land encompassed in this story — from the eastern barricade of the Gore Range to the snowfield summit of Beaver Creek Baldy.

Southwest of Vail Mountain stands the notched profile of the Mount of the Holy Cross, whose image evoked those wistful words of Longfellow: "Through all the changing scenes and seasons . . ."

This country has seen a century's worth of scenes and seasons since the Utes departed, and the survey parties measured and marveled at the land. Pioneers traversed the passes to try their hand at farming, and sheepmen followed, though none survived for long in the narrow, sharply angled valley. The land was not designed for farming or for running sheep.

But the long stretch of winter that defeated the first pioneers blessed abundantly the later ones — the pioneers of the 1960s, who found the seasons perfectly patterned for skiing. The scene changed again.

A wise, white-haired rancher, watching the recreationists pour into the county in the 1970s, spoke philosophically: "Everything can't stay like it was, and nobody would want it to. This is the most beautiful country in the world, and it should be shared. I don't see nuthin' wrong with people comin' in, though it sure done away with my old life as I've known it. But as long as there's a few cows here and there, and a coyote left to howl . . ."

Today in Vail, our lives are shaped and patterned by the land, as were the lives of all who sojourned here. We share with them the sculptured high horizons, the timbered slopes and alpenglow — our visions of the Shining Mountains.

Through all the changing scenes and seasons, the land itself endures. And still above the valley, on dark, clear winter nights — the coyotes howl.

SOURCES

THE LAST WAR TRAIL, Robert Emmitt
University of Oklahoma Press, 1954

MASSACRE, THE TRAGEDY AT WHITE RIVER, Marshall
    Sprague
University of Nebraska Press, 1975

A COLORADO READER, Editors: Carl Ubbelodhe, Maxine
    Benson, Duane A. Smith
Pruett Publishing Company, 1962, 1965, 1982

COLORADO: A LITERARY CHRONICLE, Edited, with
    Commentaries by W. Storrs Lee
Funk and Wagnalls, New York, 1970

THE GREAT GATES, Marshall Sprague
University of Nebraska Press, 1964

THE EXPLORATION OF THE COLORADO RIVER AND ITS
    CANYONS, J.W. Powell
Dover Publishing, Inc., 1961 (first published by Flood and Vincent
    in 1895 under the title Canyons of the Colorado)

GREAT SURVEYS OF THE AMERICAN WEST, Richard A.
    Bartlett
University of Oklahoma Press, 1962

HOLY CROSS, THE MOUNTAIN AND THE CITY, Robert L.
    Brown
The Caxton Printers, Ltd., Caldwell, Idaho, 1970

THE CREST OF THE CONTINENT, Ernest Ingersoll
The Rio Grande Press, Glorieta, New Mexico (first printed by R.R.
    Donnelley and Sons, Publishers, 1885)

ANNUAL REPORT OF THE UNITED STATES GEOLOGICAL
    AND GEOGRAPHICAL SURVEY OF THE TERRITORIES,
    The Exploration for the Year 1873, F.V. Hayden, United States
    Geologist
Government Printing Office, 1874

THE MAGNIFICENT ROCKIES, CREST OF A CONTINENT,
    by The Editors of American West, The Great West Series
American West Publishing Company, Palo Alto, California, 1975

YELLOWSTONE, A CENTURY OF THE WILDERNESS IDEA,
   Ann and Myron Sutton
Bonanza Books, A Chanticleer Press Edition

SNOW, Ruth Kirk
William Morrow and Company, Inc., New York 1978

THE AMAZING ADVENTURES OF LORD GORE, A TRUE
   SAGA FROM THE OLD WEST, Jack Roberts
Sundance Publications, Limited, Silverton, Colorado, 1977

WEATHER IN THE WEST, FROM THE MID CONTINENT
   TO THE PACIFIC, Bette Roda Anderson
American West Publishing Company, Palo Alto, California, 1975

TIME EXPOSURE, The Autobiography of William Henry Jackson
   Originally published: New York: Van Rees Press, 1940
University of New Mexico Press, Albuquerque

THE TIMES OF MY LIFE, Betty Ford with Chris Chase
Harper and Row and The Reader's Digest Associates, Inc., 1978

JERRY FORD UP CLOSE, AN INVESTIGATIVE
   BIOGRAPHY, Bud Vestal
Coward, McCann and Geoghegan, New York, 1974

GEARLD FORD AND THE FUTURE OF THE PRESIDENCY,
   J.F. terHorst
The Third Press, Joseph Okpaku Publishing Company, Inc., New
   York, 1974

BEAVER CREEK SKI AREA CHRONOLOGY, Paul Hauk,
   U.S.D.A. Forest Service, Retired, White River National Forest

VAIL SKI AREA CHRONOLOGY (as above)

THE FIRST VAIL SYMPOSIUM "The Role of the Mountain
   Recreation Community"
Vail, Colorado, July, 1971

INTERVIEWS

Peter Abuisi
Susan Boyd
Earl and Janet Brett
Leona Brett
Bill Brown
Byron and Vi Brown
Larry Buendorf
Cindy Bullock
Rich Caplan
Richard and Dorothy Carroll
George Caulkins
Victor and Chus de la Lama
Richard Dixon
John and Cissy Dobson
Frank and Imogene Doll
John and Diana Donovan
Bob and Patty Dorf
Earl Eaton
David Edeen
Ben Eiseman, MD
Jesse Elliot
President and Mrs. Gerald Ford
Belle Frazier
Charles Gersbach
Linda Gilbert
Frank and Marge Haas
Richard and Elvira Hammer
Joan Hannah
John Hart
Paul Hauk
Christie Hochtl
Mike and Ruth Holberg
Steve Jones
Dean Kerkling
Tom Kiahtipes
Charlie King
Debbie Kratke
Ben and Celine Krueger
Bunny Langmaid
Dave Larson
Nancy McMenamin
Jon Moller
Marie-Claire Moritz
Larry Mullin

Chupa Nelson
Bob Nichols
Edna Baldauf Norgaard
Barbara Parker
Bob Parker
Guy Parker
"Sam" Phillips
Virginia Pyke
Rhoda Rockwood
Bob Ruder
Peter Seibert
Tom Sheely
George Sisneros
Ingrid Sjorgren Giannetti
Daphne Slevin
Rod Slifer
John Smedhurst
Robert Snow
Joe Staufer
Allen Stephens
Cindy Sundberg
Jack Tweedy
Larry Walker
Bob, Ilene, and Everett Warren
Dale Williams